MW00561015

Hands On Pre-A

Table of Contents

Measurement

How Does Your Class Measure Up?

YOU WILL NEED:

- tape
- an 8' measuring tape
- a sturdy chair or stepladder
- copies of page 3

RAW DATA?!
OH, NO, NO, NO!
ALWAYS SERVE DATA
SAUTÉED WITH JUST A
HINT OF GARLIC!

OBJECTIVE: To use raw data to do the following: convert feet to inches, find an average, find difference from average, compare different groups of data, find mathematically derived statistics for athletics, use formulas to compare data

Beginning at the floor, unwind the measuring tape (with the measurement side showing) up the side of a wall. Secure it to the wall with tape. Give each student a copy of the worksheet on page 3. Have one student at a time come up to the measuring tape on the wall. Measure the height of each student and call out this measurement in feet and inches to the class. Have students fill in the name of the student and his/her height on their chart. (Remember to measure yourself, too.) After each student has been measured, have the students work individually to complete the chart. When the charts are completed, either discuss the results with the class using the questions below, or copy the questions for each student and have him/her answer them.

JUST FOR FUN:

At the end of the year, remeasure your students and write the new measurement in the last column on the worksheet. Repeat the questions. Find the average amount of growth as a class as well as each student's growth!

How Does Your Class Measure Up?

Name _____

1. What is the average height of the class? _____

2. What is the average height of the girls? _____

3. What is the average height of the boys? _____

4. Which group (on the average) is taller? _____ By how much? _____

5. How tall is your teacher? _____ By how much does the average of the class differ with the height of the teacher? _____

6. How many students measure the average height? _____

7. How many measure below average? _____

8. How many measure above average? _____

Measurement

How Does Your Class Measure Up?

Name _____

NAME	Date_____ Height (ft/in.)	Height (inches)	Differ from Average (+/-)	Date_____ Height (ft/in.)
Teacher				
Class				
	Total			

Average = total inches / # of students = _____

How Does Your Class Jump?

YOU WILL NEED:

- a gym or a room with a high ceiling
- comfortable clothing and tennis shoes
- tape
- a 12' long measuring tape
- a sturdy chair or stepladder
- copies of page 5

CAN I JUMP?!! THEY DON'T CALL ME "AIR HERSHOWITZ" FOR NUTHIN' PAL!

OBJECTIVE: To use raw data to do the following: convert feet to inches, find an average, find difference from average, compare different groups of data, find mathematically derived statistics for athletics, use formulas to compare data

Secure the measuring tape to the wall as was done in the activity "How Does Your Class Measure Up?" (page 2). The tape will need to extend 11 or 12 feet up the wall. Give each student a copy of the worksheet on page 5. Have students fill in the name of everyone in the class on the chart. Have the students come up to the measuring tape one at a time. You will need to do two measurements for each student. First, have the student stand against the wall with one arm reaching up on the tape and with his/her feet flat on the floor. This is the reach measurement. Call it out in feet and inches so students can record it in the first column on the chart. Make sure they put it next to the correct name. Next, have the same student take a two-step approach jumping at the wall and touching the highest point on the tape that he/she can. This is the jump touch measurement. Call it out loud in feet and inches and have students record the measurement.

As soon as each student has been measured for both activities and everyone has completed the first two columns of the chart, have the students work individually to complete the rest of the chart.

When the charts are complete, either discuss the results with the students asking the questions below, or copy the questions below for each student and have him/her answer them.

How Does Your Class Jump?

Name _____

1. What is the average vertical jump for the girls? _____
2. What is the average vertical jump for the boys? _____
3. Which group (on the average) has the higher vertical jump? _____ By how much? _____
4. By how much does the teacher's jump differ from the average of the class? _____

Measurement

How Does Your Class Jump?

Name _____

NAME	Reach (ft/in.)	Jump Touch (ft/in.)	Reach (in.)	Jump Touch (in.)	Vertical Jump	Differ from Av. (+/-)
Teacher						
Class						

To find vertical jump: jump touch (in.) – reach (in.) = vertical jump

Total

Average vertical jump = $\dfrac{\text{total inches vertical jump}}{\text{\# of students}}$ =

5

Wallpaper It Right!

Name _____

OBJECTIVE: To use measurements to find square feet to be covered, amount of wallpaper needed, cost of project

Use the facts below about the room to be wallpapered and the wallpaper itself to answer the questions below.

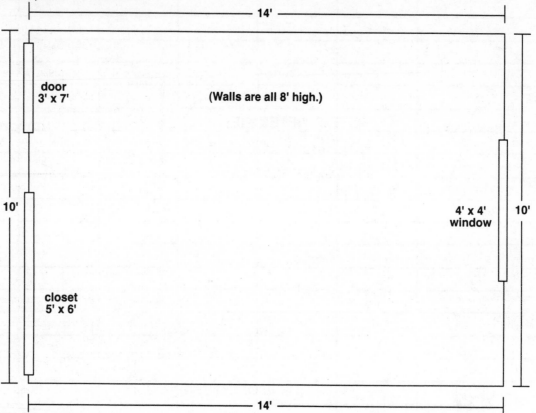

door 3' x 7'

(Walls are all 8' high.)

4' x 4' window

closet 5' x 6'

14'

10'

10'

14'

1. All of the walls are to be covered with wallpaper (excluding the closet, the door and the window!).

    a. How many square feet are to be covered? _____

    b. If the paper is sold in rolls that cover 28 square feet, how many rolls are needed? _____

    c. Each roll costs $15.98. How much money will the wallpaper cost? _____

2. Betty wants to add a border at the top that will go around the entire room.

    a. How many feet of border will she need? _____

    b. The border is sold in 5-yard rolls. How many rolls will she need? _____

    c. Each roll costs $14.99. How much will she spend on the border? _____

3. What is the total cost to wallpaper the room, including the border? _____

Metric Comparisons

Name _____

OBJECTIVES: To learn about the metric system and to be able to make comparisons between metric measurements and customary (U.S.) measurements

The metric system is made up of basic units with various prefixes to name larger or smaller units. The chart below relates the prefixes to decimal place values and powers of 10.

These units and prefixes can be used to measure length (meter—m), mass (gram—g) and capacity (liter—L). Estimating measurements will help with understanding the value of these units and how the prefixes are related.

REPEAT AFTER ME:
1 GRAM = 0.035 OZ
1 METER = 3.28 FEET
1 LITER - 33.84 OZ
NOW ISN'T THE
METRIC SYSTEM A LOT
CLEARER?

kilo	thousands
hecto	hundreds
deka	tens
no prefix	ones
deci	tenths
centi	hundredths
milli	thousandths

I. Length

One meter (1 m) is about the height of a tennis net.

One millimeter (1 mm) is about the thickness of a dime.

One centimeter (1 cm) is about the width of a large paper clip.

One kilometer (1 km) is about the length of five city blocks.

Circle the best estimate.

1. diameter of a tire   a) 66 km   b) 66 cm   c) 66 m

2. diameter of a key   a) 52 cm   b) 52 m   c) 52 mm

3. width of a doorway   a) 120 cm   b) 120 km   c) 120 mm

4. length of a football field   a) 100 m   b) 100 mm   c) 100 cm

5. distance from San Francisco to New York

   a) 4000 m   b) 4000 km   c) 4000 mm

Measurement

Metric Comparisons continued

Name _____

I. Length continued

List five items on which you see metric measurements of length.

_____

_____

_____

_____

_____

OH, THAT'S EASY! BY THE WAY, AM I HAVING A GREAT HAIR DAY OR WHAT?

II. Mass

One gram (1 g) is about the mass of a large paper clip.

One kilogram (1 kg) is about the mass of a baseball.

One milligram (1 mg) is about the mass of a grain of salt.

Circle the best mass estimate.

1.	a nickel	a) 5 mg	b) 5 g	c) 5 kg
2.	a car	a) 1000 kg	b) 1000 g	c) 1000 mg
3.	a feather	a) 17 g	b) 17 kg	c) 17 mg
4.	a pencil	a) 10 kg	b) 10 g	c) 10 mg
5.	a bowling ball	a) 7 g	b) 7 mg	c) 7 kg

List five items on which you see metric measurements of mass.

LET'S SEE, THERE'S A...UH, ER...NOPE... HOW 'BOUT A...UM, WHAT WAS THE QUESTION?

_____

_____

_____

_____

_____

III. Capacity

One eyedropper has a capacity of about one milliliter (1 mL).

The capacity of small pool is about 15 kiloliters (15 kL).

A pitcher of soda has the capacity of about one liter (1 L).

8

Metric Comparisons continued

Name _____

III. Capacity continued

Name the most reasonable unit (prefix) for measuring the following items.

1. a teaspoon of medicine _____

2. a dog's filled water bowl _____

3. a jar of pickles _____

4. a large aquarium at the zoo _____

5. a small bottle of perfume _____

5 MILLILITERS OF SUGAR HELPS THE MEDICINE GO DOWN!

List five items on which you see metric measurements of capacity.

_____
_____
_____
_____
_____

NO PROBLEM! THERE'S A... er, UM ...WELL, WHAT ABOUT...NOPE... HMM...AW, CRUD!

IV. Activities

1. Identify and discuss three items in your classroom or school that are:

   a) in length or height

   1 cm _____   1 m _____   1 mm _____
   _____   _____   _____
   _____   _____   _____

   b) in weight

   1 g _____   1 kg _____   1 mg _____
   _____   _____   _____
   _____   _____   _____

   c) in capacity

   1 mL _____   1 kL _____   1 L _____
   _____   _____   _____
   _____   _____   _____

Metric Comparisons continued

Name _____

IV. Activities continued

2. Go to the grocery store and find five items that are measured in meters, five items that are measured in grams and five items that are measured in liters. Fill in the chart below.

Item	Metric Measurement	Customary (U.S.) Measurement

You Write the Properties

YOU WILL NEED:
- 7 envelopes numbered 1-7
- 14 3" x 5" note cards cut in half (for 28 number cards)
- one copy of pages 12 and 13
- paper and pencils

THE ENVELOPE PLEASE...

OBJECTIVE: To develop the rules of the Commutative (Addition and Multiplication) Property, Associative (Addition and Multiplication) Property, Additive Identity, Multiplicative Identity and the Distributive Property by examining specific examples and formulating ideas

Copy pages 12-13 and cut them apart on the dotted lines to make seven separate instruction sheets and a main ideas/rules sheet. Put the instructions in each respective envelope. Also include the following in the envelopes :

AND THE WINNER IS...

Envelope 1—four different numbers written on the note cards (Pick any numbers, i.e. 0, 5, 31, 64.)

Envelope 2—four different numbers written on the note cards

Envelope 3—the number 0, a variable (i.e. x) and two different numbers written on note cards

Envelope 4—four different numbers written on note cards

Envelope 5—four different numbers written on note cards

Envelope 6—the number 1, a variable and two different numbers written on note cards

Envelope 7—four different numbers written on note cards

Divide the students into groups of two to three. Give each group an envelope containing the above materials and a copy of main ideas/rules (page 13). Make sure each student has pencil and paper. Groups should be given three minutes with each envelope. This activity will allow students to experiment with numbers and write the following properties in their own words :

...ME! I'D LIKE TO THANK ALL THE PEOPLE WHO...

Envelope 1—Commutative for Addition
Envelope 2—Associative for Addition
Envelope 3—Additive Identity
Envelope 4—Commutative for Multiplication
Envelope 5—Associative for Multiplication
Envelope 6—Multiplicative Identity
Envelope 7—Distributive Property

When each group has completed each envelope, discuss and compare the actual properties. Have students explain to you and each other what they think the property in each envelope might be.

You Write the Properties continued

#1 Instructions

1. Pick two numbers and add them. Write down the exact sequence in which they were added and their sum. Change the order of the two numbers and repeat instructions. Label this **Series 1** on your paper.

2. Pick three numbers. Repeat Step 1. Label this **Series 2**.

3. Pick four numbers. Repeat Step 1. Label this **Series 3**.

4. Review all information you wrote down for each series and describe the sum. Write a sentence that explains what is happening. What is the main idea?

Note: There will be several ways to change Series 2 and 3. Try them all!

#2 Instructions

1. Pick three numbers and write them down. Put parentheses around two and add them first. Then, add the third number. Write down the exact sequence, placement of parentheses and the sum.

2. Keep the three numbers in the same sequence but change the placement of the parentheses. Find the sum. Write this down.

3. Repeat Steps 1 and 2 using three different numbers. Record all information.

4. Review all information you wrote down for each series and describe the sum. Write a sentence that explains what is happening. What is the main idea?

#3 Instructions

1. Pick a number and add zero to it. Record the sum.

2. Repeat this process with each number writing down the pattern each time.

3. Add zero to the variable and record the sum.

4. Review the information for each series and describe the sum. Write a sentence that explains what is happening. What is the main idea?

#4 Instructions

1. Pick two numbers and multiply them. Write down the exact sequence in which they were multiplied and their product. Change the order of the two numbers and repeat instructions. Label this **Series 1** on your paper.

2. Pick three numbers. Repeat Step 1. Label this **Series 2**.

3. Pick four numbers. Repeat Step 1. Label this **Series 3**.

4. Review all information you wrote down for each series and describe the product. Write a sentence that explains what is happening. What is the main idea?

Note: There will be several ways to change Series 2 and 3. Try them all!

You Write the Properties continued

#5 Instructions

1. Pick three numbers and write them down. Put parentheses around two and multiply them first. Then, multiply the product by the third number. Write down the exact sequence, placement of parentheses and the product.

2. Keep the three numbers in the same sequence but change the placement of the parentheses. Find the product. Write this down.

3. Repeat Steps 1 and 2 using three different numbers. Record all information.

4. Review all information you write down for each series and describe the product. Write a sentence that explains what is happening. What is the main idea?

#6 Instructions

1. Pick a number and multiply it by one. Record the product.

2. Repeat this process with each number writing down the pattern each time.

3. Multiply one by the variable and record the product.

4. Review the information for each series and describe the product. Write a sentence that explains what is happening. What is the main idea?

#7 Instructions

1. Pick three numbers and place them in this expression: ___ (___ + ___). Add the two numbers in parentheses. Then, multiply that sum by the outside number.

2. Take these same three numbers in the same order and multiply the first number by the second number. Then, multiply the first by the third and add the two products.

3. Use three different numbers and repeat Steps 1 and 2.

4. Review the recorded information and compare the final answer in each series. Write a sentence that explains what is happening. What is the main idea?

Main Ideas/Rules

Envelope 1 _____

Envelope 2 _____

Envelope 3 _____

Envelope 4 _____

Envelope 5 _____

Envelope 6 _____

Envelope 7 _____

Survey Project

OBJECTIVES: To develop and complete survey questions and analysis and to use frequency tables, bar graphs, circle graphs and discussion to finalize and describe findings

Each student will survey between 50 and 100 people and organize the data using basic number properties, percents and some elementary statistical tools. To do this, the student must:

1. Decide on a question (topic) that has four or five possible answers.
   Example: Of the following colors, which do you like best?
   a. red
   b. blue
   c. orange
   d. black
   e. purple

2. Prepare a tally/frequency chart to use for his/her survey. (See example to the right using the above question.)

	Tally	Frequency	% of Total
1. red	⊮ II	7	15%
2. blue	⊮ ⊮ I	11	24%
3. orange	II	2	5%
4. black	⊮ III	8	17%
5. purple	⊮ ⊮ ⊮ III	18	39%
	Total	46	

Make sure you go over the given example with the students so that they have a good idea of what you want them to do. Remind students that when getting their percents, they must round. Tell students that the total percent must equal 100, so they must be extra careful when rounding.

Give each student a copy of page 15. Then, either give students a copy of the following directions, or read them to the students to help them complete the worksheet.

Directions for Survey Project

1. Decide on a question for your survey. Remember: The question must have four or five possible answers. Fill in your question on page 15.

2. Ask between 50 and 100 people your question. Tally the responses in the table.

3. When you have finished gathering the responses, add up each tally and write that number in the frequency column on the table. Total the frequencies. This number represents how many people you surveyed.

4. Divide each frequency by the total to get a percent for each response.

5. Make a bar graph to show the responses.

6. Make a circle graph to show the percent for each response.

7. Write a paragraph describing your question, the results of the survey (be specific using percents, etc.) and any general comments.

8. Write a series of questions to "quiz" your classmates on your results. Share this information either in a written or oral presentation.

Survey Project

Name _____

Question: _____

_____

_____

Table:

Response	Tally	Frequency	% of Total
1.			
2.			
3.			
4.			
5.			
Total			

Bar Graph: Circle Graph:

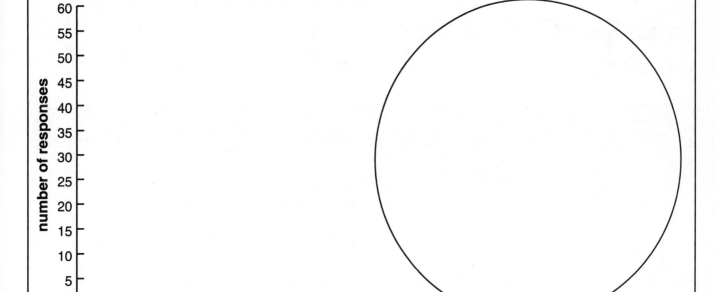

Making Change

Numbers

YOU WILL NEED:

a variety of chips or play money for students

OBJECTIVE: To use problem-solving skills (patterns) and number combinations to answer the activity's question

> OUR SPECIAL TODAY IS THREE QUARTERS FOR A BUCK... YOU WANT FRIES WITH THAT?

Ask students how many ways they think change can be made for a one dollar bill without using pennies. (Nickels, dimes, quarters and half dollars can be used.) Discuss their guesses and see which student came closest (or had) the correct answer of 40.

Break your class into cooperative learning groups. Give each group an abundance of colored chips. Tell students that each color of chip represents a coin (i.e. red = dimes, blue = nickels, etc.). Have the groups race to find all 40 ways to make change for a one dollar bill. Give each group of students a copy of the chart below to use to record their answers as they work.

When the groups are finished, see if any used patterns to quicken their task. Have the groups share their ideas and strategies in solving the problem.

Group Members _____

5¢ 10¢ 25¢ 50¢	5¢ 10¢ 25¢ 50¢	5¢ 10¢ 25¢ 50¢	5¢ 10¢ 25¢ 50¢
1. __ __ __ __	11. __ __ __ __	21. __ __ __ __	31. __ __ __ __
2. __ __ __ __	12. __ __ __ __	22. __ __ __ __	32. __ __ __ __
3. __ __ __ __	13. __ __ __ __	23. __ __ __ __	33. __ __ __ __
4. __ __ __ __	14. __ __ __ __	24. __ __ __ __	34. __ __ __ __
5. __ __ __ __	15. __ __ __ __	25. __ __ __ __	35. __ __ __ __
6. __ __ __ __	16. __ __ __ __	26. __ __ __ __	36. __ __ __ __
7. __ __ __ __	17. __ __ __ __	27. __ __ __ __	37. __ __ __ __
8. __ __ __ __	18. __ __ __ __	28. __ __ __ __	38. __ __ __ __
9. __ __ __ __	19. __ __ __ __	29. __ __ __ __	39. __ __ __ __
10. __ __ __ __	20. __ __ __ __	30. __ __ __ __	40. __ __ __ __

Numbers

The Answer Is the Problem
(Addition and Subtraction)

Name _Emily_ ♡

OBJECTIVE: To take a reverse approach to solving math equations (as when the answer is given and the correct problem must be written)

Sometimes all we know is the answer to a problem. Figuring out the pieces is a problem in itself! Practice a few of these kinds of problems on your own below and on pages 18-19. Then, make up some problems to share with a classmate. The ones below deal with exclusively addition and subtraction.

In each problem below, you can use only three of the four given numbers in the box. You must also insert the addition (+) and subtraction (—) signs!

$$\boxed{12, 5, 3, 15}$$

Example: __15__ + __3__ – __12__ = 6

1. __15__ – __12__ – __3__ = 0
2. __15__ – __12__ + __5__ = 8
3. __12__ + __5__ – __15__ = 2
4. __12__ + __5__ + __3__ = 20
5. __15__ – __5__ – __3__ = 7
6. __15__ – __5__ + __3__ = 13

Can you come up with more than one solution for a certain answer? Make up six of your own. Trade with a classmate and solve each other's. Remember to give the numbers to use in the box and the answers. Only use addition and subtraction.

$$\boxed{3, 5, 1, 4}$$

1. __3__ + __5__ – __3__ = __5__
2. __5__ + __5__ – __4__ = __6__
3. __5__ + __1__ + __4__ = __10__
4. __3__ – __5__ + __4__ = __2__
5. __4__ – __5__ + __1__ = __0__
6. __3__ + __4__ + __5__ = __12__

17

The Answer Is the Problem
(All Four Operations)

Numbers

Name _____

OBJECTIVE: To take a reverse approach to solving math equations (as when the answer is given and the correct problem must be written)

Now, try some problems involving all four operations. The answers as well as the operations are provided below. Remember: You can use three of the four given numbers in the box.

$$\boxed{2, 3, 4, 6}$$

Example: __4__ x __3__ + __6__ = 18

1. ____ x ____ ÷ ____ = 1

2. ____ x ____ − ____ = 5

3. ____ ÷ ____ x ____ = 6

4. ____ x ____ ÷ ____ = 8

5. ____ x ____ − ____ = 14

6. ____ x ____ + ____ = 15

Can you come up with more than one solution for a certain answer? Make up six of your own. Trade with a classmate and solve each other's. Remember to give the numbers to use in the box. Also, provide the operations and the answers.

$$\boxed{\text{____, ____, ____, ____}}$$

1. ____ ____ ____ = ____

2. ____ ____ ____ = ____

3. ____ ____ ____ = ____

4. ____ ____ ____ = ____

5. ____ ____ ____ = ____

6. ____ ____ ____ = ____

Numbers

The Answer Is the Problem (Fractions)

Name _____

OBJECTIVE: To take a reverse approach to solving math equations (as when the answer is given and the correct problem must be written)

The same type of problems as found on pages 17 and 18 can also be done using fractions! Using any two of the four given fractions, see if you can write the problems.

$$\frac{7}{12} \ , \ \frac{5}{12} \ , \ \frac{1}{12} \ , \ \frac{11}{12}$$

Example: $\dfrac{\frac{5}{12}}{\ } \ + \ \dfrac{\frac{11}{12}}{\ } \ = \ 1\frac{1}{3}$

1. _____ − _____ = $\frac{1}{2}$

2. _____ + _____ = 1

3. _____ − _____ = $\frac{1}{6}$

4. _____ + _____ = $1\frac{1}{2}$

5. _____ − _____ = $\frac{1}{3}$

6. _____ + _____ = $\frac{2}{3}$

Challenge: (Use all four numbers.)

_____ + _____ − _____ − _____ = 0

Can you come up with more than one solution for a certain answer? Make up six of your own. Trade with a classmate and solve each other's. Remember to give the fractions to use in the box. Also, provide the operations and the answers.

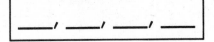

1. _____ _____ = _____

2. _____ _____ = _____

3. _____ _____ _____ = _____

4. _____ _____ = _____

5. _____ _____ _____ = _____

6. _____ _____ _____ = _____

Numbers

The Answer Is the Puzzle
(Addition and Subtraction)

Name _____

OBJECTIVE: To take a reverse approach to solving math equations (as when the answer is given and the correct problem must be written)

Cut out the boxes with the numbers in them in the bottom right corner of the page. Use these numbers to fill in each puzzle so that each column and row produces the given answer. After you have completed the puzzles, copy the answers down on another piece of paper. Challenge someone outside your class to complete the puzzles!

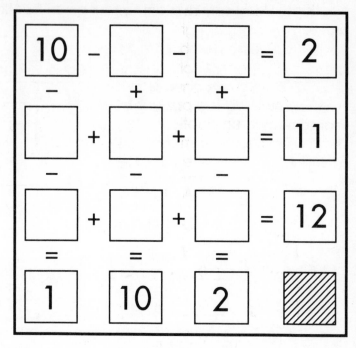

THE PROBLEM IS THAT I DON'T KNOW THE ANSWERS!

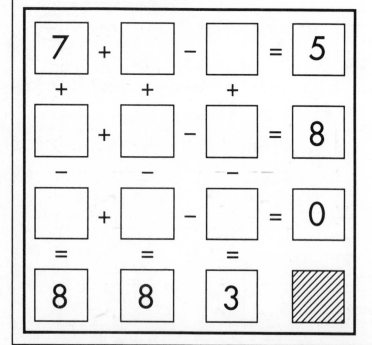

20 ©Instructional Fair, Inc.

Numbers

The Answer Is the Puzzle
(All Four Operations)

Name _____

OBJECTIVE: To take a reverse approach to solving math equations (as when the answer is given and the correct problem must be written)

Cut out the boxes with the numbers in them in the bottom right corner of the page. Use these numbers to fill in each puzzle so that each column and row produces the given answer. After you have completed the puzzles, copy the answers down on another piece of paper. Challenge someone outside your class to complete the puzzles!

AREN'T NUMBERS FUN?!

9	x ☐	+ ☐	= 16
x	x	x	
☐	x ☐	+ ☐	= 38
÷	÷	÷	
☐	x ☐	+ ☐	= 10
=	=	=	
15	3	14	▨

5	x ☐	÷ ☐	= 10
x	+	+	
☐	x ☐	÷ ☐	= 18
÷	−	+	
☐	+ ☐	− ☐	= 4
=	=	=	
6	6	13	▨

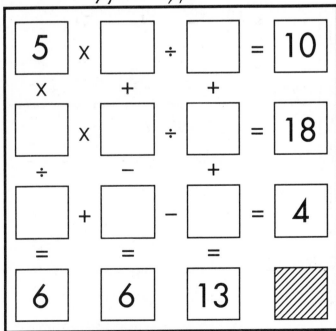

2	4	6	8	10
2	4	6	8	10
2	4	6	8	10
1	3	5	7	9
1	3	5	7	9
1	3	5	7	9

Golf Field Trip

Name _____

OBJECTIVE: To use logic and problem-solving skills to find solutions

Teeing Off

Sally, a math student, takes a field trip to the local golf course. She is a very exact person who always hits the ball well and sends it exactly one of three distances—60, 90 or 150 yards. The ball always goes straight toward the hole, passes over the hole, or drops in the cup. What is the best (lowest) score she could get on the nine holes she is playing?

*The score per hole is the number of shots it takes to get the ball in the cup.

SCORE CARD		
HOLE	YARDS	SCORE
1	210	
2	240	
3	180	
4	120	
5	360	
6	330	
7	300	
8	270	
9	420	
TOTAL SCORE		

GOLF... THE FINAL FRONTIER!

Visit to the Pro Shop

Sally's friend Brenda doesn't golf, but she loves to shop. She stays in the Pro Shop and spends $175. She buys a hat, a jacket and an umbrella. Exactly what else can she buy with her money if she spends the rest of it?

CAN I HELP YOU?

PRO SHOP

HAT .... $10.00   T-SHIRT $15.00

JACKET .... $54.00   SWEATSHIRT $20.00

UMBRELLA .... $13.00   SHORTS $13.00

COFFEE MUG ..... $6.00   POSTER $3.00

POST CARD .... $1.00   SOCKS $4.00

RAINCOAT $41.00

22

Tangrams

YOU WILL NEED:

- overhead transparencies
- overhead tangrams

TANGRAM FOR MR. RIDER, TANGRAM FOR MR. RIDER... OH... ER, UH...SORRY, THAT'S TELEGRAM FOR MR. RIDER, TELEGRAM FOR MR. RIDER!

OBJECTIVE: To use tangrams to create various mathematical and non-mathematical pictures; Different patterns and visual problem solving will be explored.

The tangram is a geometric puzzle used to form various figures. This is a great way to get students working with shapes. Use the overhead tangrams to show students the tangram puzzle put together. Then, take the puzzle apart, piece by piece, and explain each piece. Show students how the pieces can fit together to form other figures.

Give each student a copy of the puzzle on the bottom of page 24. Have the students cut apart the tangram puzzle into seven pieces on the solid lines. Using the seven pieces, have the students put them back together to make the square. Next, put the figures below and on the top of page 24 on the overhead or make a copy for each student. Have the students recreate each figure. When students are proficient using the pieces, have them create their own designs and exchange them with other students.

Tangrams

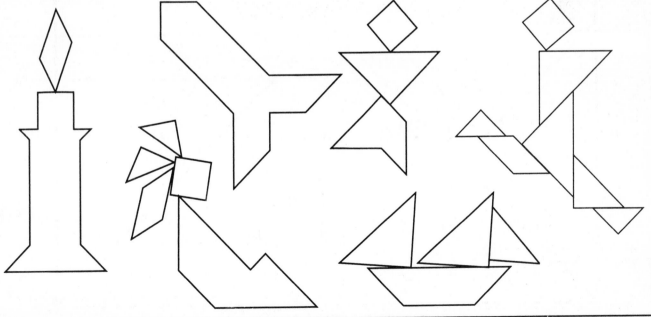

Tangrams continued

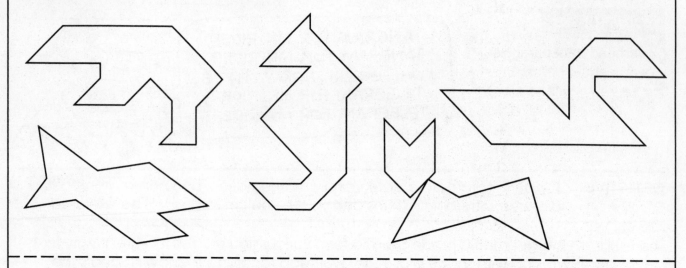

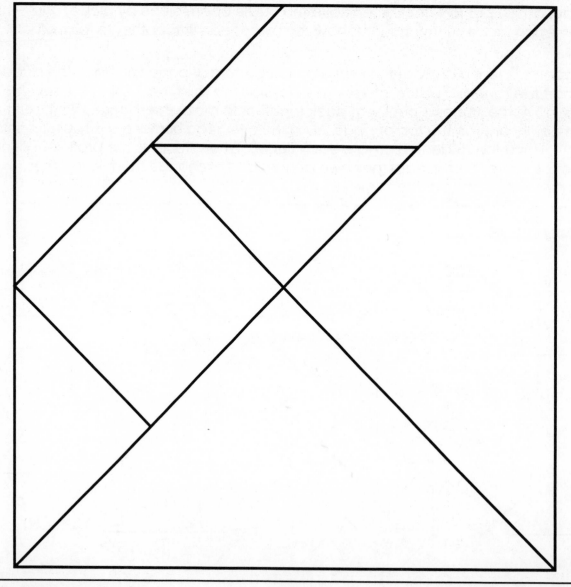

How Many?

Name _____

OBJECTIVE: To use counting, patterns and logic to solve brainteasers

Answer these four puzzles carefully!

1. Draw two squares to divide the large square into nine sections with exactly one dot in each section.

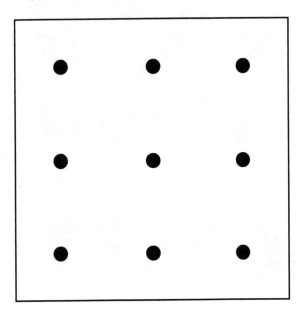

2. Find the total number of triangles.

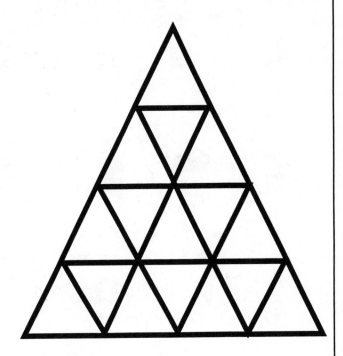

3. Find the total number of squares.

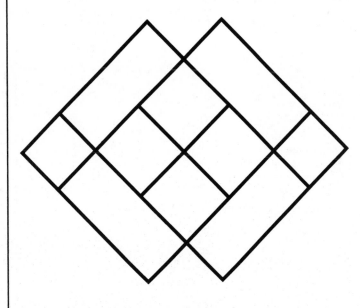

4. Sue is making flash cards out of a piece of posterboard with the dimensions of 22" x 28". She wants each flash card to be 2" x 4". How many flash cards can she cut from one piece of posterboard?

1 Is to 2 as 3 Is to ? (A)

Name _____

OBJECTIVES: To explore spatial relationships and to practice finding, drawing and creating shape challenges

In the problems below, shape 2 is changed in a certain way from shape 1. Shape 3 is similar to shape 1. What will the next shape look like if shape 3 is changed in the same way? Circle the correct answer.

1. is to   as   is to
   1   2   3   A   B   C   D   E

2. is to   as   is to
   1   2   3   A   B   C   D   E

3. is to   as   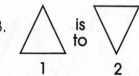 is to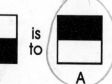
   1   2   3   A   B   C   D   E

4. is to   as   is to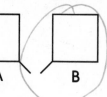
   1   2   3   A   B   C   D   E

Draw what the next shape should look like.

5. is to   as   is to
   1   2   3

6. is to   as   is to
   1   2   3

Create three of your own shape changes. Trade with classmates and challenge them.

Shapes

1 Is to 2 as 3 Is to ? (B)

Name _____

OBJECTIVES: To explore spatial relationships and to practice finding, drawing and creating shape challenges

In the following problems, shape 2 is changed in a certain way from shape 1. Shape 3 is similar to shape 1. What will the next shape look like if shape 3 is changed in the same way? Circle the correct answer.

1. is to as 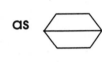 is to

   1   2   3   A   B   C   D   E

2. is to as is to

   1   2   3   A   B   C   D   E

3. is to as is to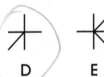

   1   2   3   A   B   C   D   E

4. is to as 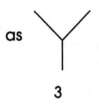 is to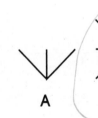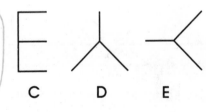

   1   2   3   A   B   C   D   E

Draw what the next shape should look like.

5. 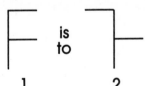 is to as is to

   1   2   3

6. is to as is to

   1   2   3

Create three of your own shape changes. Trade with classmates and challenge them.

Box It Up (A)

Name _____

OBJECTIVE: To use shapes and visual problem-solving skills to fit pieces into puzzles

Cut out the eight shapes at the bottom of the page. These shapes were formed using one, two, three or four squares of the given 5 x 5 grid. Cover the 5 x 5 grid using all of the eight shapes. Is there more than one way it can be covered? Check with your classmates and compare answers.

The Square

The Shapes
(Can be turned or flipped.)

Box It Up (B)

Name _____

OBJECTIVE: To use shapes and visual problem-solving skills to fit pieces into puzzles

The Rectangle

Cut out the nine shapes at the bottom of the page. These shapes were formed using one, two, three, four or five squares of the given 6 x 5 grid. Cover the 6 x 5 grid using all of the nine shapes. Is there more than one way it can be covered? Check with your classmates and compare answers.

The Shapes (Can be turned or flipped.)

Shapes Around School

OBJECTIVE: To use a hands-on approach to study various mathematical shapes and patterns

After learning the mathematical facts about geometric shapes, it is helpful for students to see the reality of these shapes used in everyday things. Take your class on a quick "field trip" through your school. On the field trip, students are to look for the shapes listed below "in action." Give each student a copy of the activity below. Students are to list things that they see around the school under each shape's name (i.e. face of a locker is a rectangle).

When the field trip is over, discuss the results with the class. See if students came up with the same or different answers. Then, ask students questions to expand on this thinking such as, "Are there shapes outside (natural)? What professions will involve working with a lot of different shapes?" As an assignment, have the students do the same basic activity during an after-school activity (i.e. at an athletic event, working in a mall, grocery shopping, etc.). A field trip to an architecture company would help students see professionals in action who actually work with shapes.

- -

Shapes Around School

Name _____

List items that are, or contain, the following shapes.

Circle	Semicircle	Square	Rectangle	Triangle	Rhombus
Yoga ball t.v. reception lego dish	red weights	file drawer	Picture frame t.v.		

Trapezoid	Parallelogram	Pentagon	Hexagon	Octagon
lamp shade			weight	

Teacher for the Day (Class Summary)

OBJECTIVES: To use a numerical study to collect, organize and analyze data from a teacher's grade book; To make comparisons, find averages, assign letter grades and present a written and visual analysis of the class

Give each student copies of the bottom of this page and pages 32-34. In this activity, students are going to complete the grade book (page 32) and analyze the data in the grade book by answering the questions on the worksheets.

- -

Teacher for the Day (Class Summary)

Name _____

1. Using page 32, find the cumulative total at the end of each week for each student. Use this total to find each student's percent and grade. Use the scale to the right to assign grades.

   To find the percent, divide the student's total points by the total points possible. Round to the nearest tenth. Then, apply the scale.

89.5 →	100+	A
79.5 →	89.4	B
69.5 →	79.4	C
59.5 →	69.4	D
59.4	below	F

TABLE A

	# of students	% of class
A		
B		
C		
D		
F		
	20	

2. Complete Table A using the grade book results.

3. Using the results from Table A, make a bar graph showing the number of students receiving each letter grade. (Use colored pencils for the graph.)

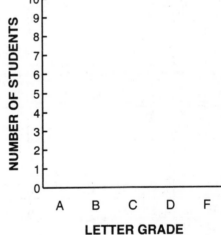

4. Make a circle graph showing the breakdown of percentages in the table. (Use colored pencils for the graph.)

5. On the back of this page, write a summary, or analysis, of your class results.

31

Teacher for the Day (Grade Book)

Name _____

Block 1 (top)

Student	M (5)	T (100)	W BONUS (3)	Th (10)	F (5)	Total	%	Grade
Sue	3	80	1	7	5			
Jim	3	75	1	6	4			
Bob	5	98	2	8	5			
Gail	5	81	0	7	4			
Steve	3	64	0	5	3			
Pam	4	87	2	8	4			
Cathy	5	93	3	7	5			
Earl	3	80	1	6	5			
John	5	93	2	8	4			
Jane	4	88	1	9	4			
Sam	4	75	1	8	3			
Julie	5	94	3	10	5			
Paul	3	61	0	7	3			
Scott	3	54	1	6	2			
Carly	3	63	0	6	3			
Kevin	1	58	0	4	1			
Kristin	4	97	3	7	4			
Jack	4	93	2	6	5			
Stacy	5	84	1	8	4			
Molly	5	99	3	10	5			

Block 2

Student	M (5)	T (15)	W (5)	Th (50)	F (10)
Sue	5	13	4	40	8
Jim	3	12	4	43	7
Bob	5	14	4	49	9
Gail	4	11	4	46	8
Steve	3	10	3	31	5
Pam	3	12	4	45	8
Cathy	5	13	5	50	8
Earl	4	9	3	42	7
John	4	15	5	39	8
Jane	5	14	4	48	9
Sam	4	11	4	37	8
Julie	3	14	3	49	10
Paul	3	9	3	31	6
Scott	4	10	3	38	7
Carly	3	9	4	39	7
Kevin	2	11	3	30	4
Kristin	4	13	4	46	9
Jack	3	15	4	49	8
Stacy	4	13	5	39	9
Molly	5	15	5	50	10

Block 3

Student	M (5)	T (75)	W	Th (10)	F (10)
Sue	5	70		4	6
Jim	2	60		7	7
Bob	5	73		9	9
Gail	3	65		8	8
Steve	2	51		7	5
Pam	4	71		8	7
Cathy	5	74		10	9
Earl	4	67		8	6
John	4	73		9	9
Jane	4	66		8	9
Sam	3	58		8	7
Julie	4	73		10	10
Paul	2	51		5	8
Scott	3	60		6	7
Carly	2	60		7	6
Kevin	2	57		6	3
Kristin	4	72		6	9
Jack	5	68		7	9
Stacy	3	71		8	7
Molly	5	74		10	10

Block 4 (bottom) — Cumulative Possible Points

Student	M (10)	T (5)	W (5)	Th (30)	F (5)
Sue	8	3	5	29	4
Jim	7	5	4	25	3
Bob	10	5	5	29	4
Gail	6	4	4	23	4
Steve	4	2	3	18	4
Pam	8	4	4	26	4
Cathy	9	5	4	28	4
Earl	7	3	4	21	3
John	9	4	4	28	4
Jane	7	4	2	25	3
Sam	8	4	5	19	4
Julie	10	5	5	30	5
Paul	3	2	1	15	3
Scott	6	3	3	19	4
Carly	7	3	3	21	3
Kevin	5	3	2	19	3
Kristin	10	3	4	30	4
Jack	9	4	4	28	4
Stacy	8	4	4	27	5
Molly	10	5	5	30	5

Teacher for the Day (Specifics)

Name _____

Answer the following questions based on the grade book results.

1. Progress Reports were sent after the first two weeks to students earning a 65% or below. List the students (if any) who received progress reports along with their percentages.

   _____

2. a. What was the average number of points after the first week? _____

   b. Who had the highest number of points? _____ How many? _____
      What percentage was this? _____

   c. Who had the lowest number of points? _____ How many? _____
      What percentage was this? _____

3. a. What was the average grade on the 30-point test in the first week? _____

   b. Which students were closest to the average?_____

4. a. What was the average number of points after the second week? _____

   b. Who had the highest number of points? _____ How many? _____
      What percentage was this? _____ Was it the same students as week 1?

      _____

   c. Who had the lowest number of points? _____ How many? _____
      What percentage was this? _____ Was it the same student as week 1? _____

5. a. What was the average grade on the 100-point test in the fourth week? _____

   b. Which student was closest to the average? _____

6. a. Of those receiving Progress Reports, which students (if any) improved their grades by the end of the fourth week?_____

   b. Which of those students dropped their grades?_____

   c. What did each of these students receive for that grading period?_____

      _____

7. a. Drop the 50-point test in the third week from each student's points (Adjust the total points possible!) and refigure the grades. Do this on the grade book on page 32 in the last three columns.

   b. How many students' letter grades changed? _____

   c. How many percentages were raised? _____ Whose? _____

      _____

   d. How many percentages were lowered? _____ Whose?_____

      _____

   e. Whose stayed the same? _____

Teacher for the Day
(Battle of the Sexes)

Name _____

Analyze the students' grades according to those earned by girls and those earned by boys.

1. Complete the following table from your class results (not counting subtracting out the 50-point test).

	total #	# of girls	# of boys	% of class	% of % girls	% of % boys
A						
B						
C						
D						
F						
	20	10	10			

2. Use the table to make a bar graph showing the total number of students receiving each letter grade as well as the breakdown of boy and girl grades for each letter. (Example:)

3. Use the table to make a circle graph showing both the comparison of percent of each grade earned and grades earned of boys and girls. (Hint: Use a different color for each grade. Within grades, use dots for girls and stripes for boys. Ex:)

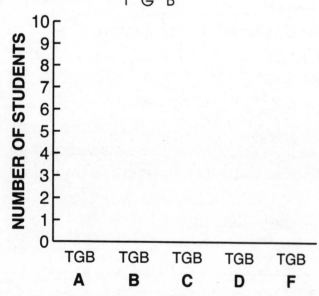

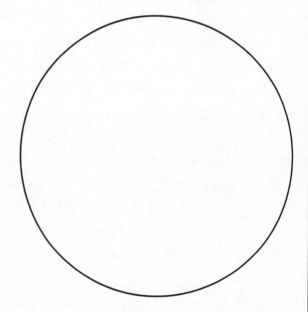

4. On the back of this page, write an analysis of the comparison of boys' grades and girls' grades from your class results.

Basic Counting Principle

OBJECTIVES: To develop the Basic Counting Principle using tree diagrams as a visual tool; To make tree diagrams, list possible outcomes and find the number of possible outcomes

One of the most important aspects of probability is the number of possible outcomes. Making a tree diagram of information will help the students develop an understanding of the number of possible outcomes (and how to find it) and what the actual outcomes are.

Discuss probability with the students. Go over the example below with them and explain each step and why you are doing each step. Then, give students a copy of page 36 to complete on their own.

Example:

A typical probability question involves flipping one or more coins.

Question: How many ways can three coins land?

HEADS, YOU DO THE PROBLEM, TAILS, YOU DO THE PROBLEM! HEY— NO PROBLEM!

Tree Diagram

The idea of a tree diagram is to "map out" what could happen.

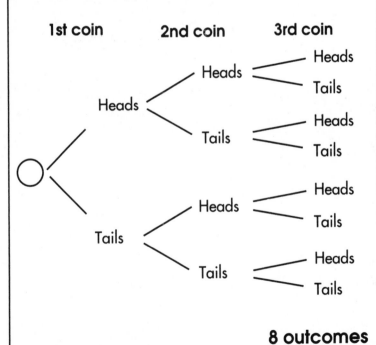

8 outcomes

Outcomes

The first coin could land on heads, the second on tails and the third on heads (HTH).

The eight outcomes are:

HHH	HHT	
HTH	HTT	= ⑧
THH	THT	
TTH	TTT	

Basic Counting Principle

The Basic Counting Principle says to multiply the number of ways each event can happen. In the coin example, there are two ways the first coin can land, two ways the second coin can land and two ways the third coin can land.

$$2 \times 2 \times 2 = 8$$

Basic Counting Principle continued

Name _____

1. Make a tree diagram to show how many different outfits a businessman will have if he packs two suits, three ties and two hats. State the actual outcomes, and verify the number using a tree diagram and the Basic Counting Principle.

Tree Diagram

Outcomes

Basic Counting Principle

2. How many sundaes (one ice cream, one sauce and one topping) can be made with vanilla and strawberry ice cream, fudge and butterscotch sauces and peanut and chocolate chip toppings?

Tree Diagram

Outcomes

Basic Counting Principle

Probability (Flip a Coin)

YOU WILL NEED:

a coin, a copy of the bottom of this page for every group of two or three students

WHAT'S THE PROBABILITY OF LIFE ON OTHER PLANETS? OFFHAND, I'D SAY IT'S PRETTY DARN GOOD!

OBJECTIVES: To explore the basic concept of probability with hands-on learning using coins; To use charts to organize and explain the results

Divide students into groups of two or three. Give each group a coin and a copy of the chart below. Each group will flip a coin and record the results (in tally form) on the chart. Arrange so that a few of the groups flip a coin 50 times, a few flip 75 times and a few flip 100 times. (Hint: Have one student flip the coin, another one record the data and the other one count the number of flips.)

When the groups have finished, have them record the total number of heads, tails and flips. Students then divide the number of heads by the total number of flips. The answer should be recorded as a simplified fraction and as a percent in the spaces provided on the chart. This process should be repeated by the students using the number of tails.

Use this data to introduce basic probability ideas. Compare each group's fractions and percents. Then, discuss some things with students such as, "Are the groups' numbers similar to each other? What percent are they close to? Did the number of times a coin was flipped have any effect on the numbers? Why do sports events have a coin toss to determine side of field? What is the probability of getting tails? heads?"

Flip a Coin   Group Members _____

	HEADS	TAILS	
			total # of flips
Total	(H)	(T)	
	_____ ___%	_____ ___%	

Probability (Flip Two Coins)

YOU WILL NEED:

2 coins, a copy of the bottom of this page for every group of two or three students

WHAT'S THE ODDS OF THIS PAGE DRIVING YOU NUTS?

OBJECTIVES: To explore the basic concept of probability with hands-on learning using coins; To use charts to organize and explain their results

Divide students into groups of two or three. Give each group two coins and a copy of the chart below. Each group will flip two coins and record the results (in tally form) on the chart. Arrange it so that a few of the groups flip two coins 50 times, a few flip 75 times and a few flip 100 times. (Hint: Have one student flip the coin, another one record the data and the other one count the number of flips.)

When the groups have finished, have them record the total number of two heads, two tails, one head and one tail, and flips. Students then divide each of these totals by the total number of flips and record the answer as a simplified fraction and as a percent. The fractions and percents should be written on the chart in the spaces provided.

Use this data to discuss probability concepts with the students. Compare each group's data. Ask students questions similar to, "What do the fractions add up to? Is this important? What does it mean? Did the number of times the coins were flipped have any effect? What is the probability of getting two heads? two tails? one head and one tail?"

Flip Two Coins

Group Members _____

	Two Heads	Two Tails	One Head, One Tail	
				total # of flips
Total	(HH)	(TT)	(HT)	
	____ ___%	____ ___%	____ ___%	

Probability (M&M Research)

YOU WILL NEED:

one copy of the bottom of this page per student, one large bag of plain or peanut M&M's, paper plates

HEY—THESE ARE PRETTY DARN TASTY!

OBJECTIVE: To explore the basic concept of probability with hands-on learning using M&M's; To use charts to organize and explain the results

---

Divide the students into groups of three or four. Give each group a paper plate filled with a random pouring from the bag of M&M's and a copy of the table below. Students should begin filling in the second column on the table by first counting their inventory on their paper plate.

Next, have students determine the probability (column 3) of selecting an M&M from each category (color). To do this, students divide the number of that color by the total number of M&M's on their plate and simplify. Ask students what they think the sum of probabilities should equal (one). Ask them to explain why this is so. Then, discuss if there are more of certain colors than others and what effect this will have on the probability of certain colors.

Generalize one step further and describe probability as the percent chance of something happening (column 4). Ask students if the percent chance column totals 100%. Have each student in each group eat two M&M's and repeat the activities.

M&M Research   Group Members _____

Color	Number	Probability	% Chance
red			
yellow			
orange			
light brown			
dark brown			
green			
TOTAL			

Probability (Roll a Die)

YOU WILL NEED:

a die, one copy of the bottom of this page for every group of two or three students

> SNAKE EYES!!

OBJECTIVES: To explore the basic concept of probability with hands-on learning using dice; To use charts to organize and explain their results

Divide students into groups of two or three. Give each group a die and a copy of the chart below. Through these activities, students will develop ideas for basic probability concepts.

Have each group roll one die 50 times and record the results (in tally form) on the chart. After the die has been rolled 50 times, have the students complete column 3 (total number).

Students should then determine the probability of rolling each number. To do this, divide the total number column of each die number by 50. Compare each group's information. Ask students if they are all about $\frac{1}{6}$? Why do they think this is so? Ask them what the sum of the probability is (should be about one). Ask them to explain why this is so. Next, have the students find the percent chance of each event. Students should add the percent chance. Ask them what the sum is and why (100%).

Discuss each group's findings and use the patterns to generalize and expand probability to other topics (i.e. spinning a spinner with various areas marked on it, picking a number out of a hat, etc.). See if your class can come up with other projects to do to explore "chances."

Roll a Die

Group Members _____

Die Number	Tally of Times	Total #	Probability	% Chance
1				
2				
3				
4				
5				
6				
TOTAL		50		

Probability (What Have You Learned?)

Name _____

1. Make a tree diagram and state the possible sandwiches if Billy makes one with one meat, one sauce and one bread type from the menu below. Use the letters in parentheses to help you.

meat
roast beef (R)
turkey (T)
bologna (B)

sauce
mayonnaise (M)
mustard (Y)

bread
sourdough (S)
whole wheat (W)
white (P)

Tree Diagram

Possible Sandwiches

Basic Counting Principle

How many different sandwiches can Billy make?

_____

2. What is the probability of getting tails on a coin toss? _____

3. What is the probability of getting a heads and a tails when tossing two coins?

_____

4. What is the probability of rolling a 5 on a die? _____

5. If you roll one die, pick it up and roll it again, what is the probability of getting a one and then a 6? _____

6. If you spin the spinner shown:

   a. what is the probability of spinning a blue? _____

   b. what is the probability of spinning a red or a green? _____

   c. what is the probability of spinning orange? _____

Statistics

Probability (What Have You Learned?) continued

Name _____

7. If you have three green, two brown, four red and seven orange M&M's, what is the probability of selecting a red? _____

8. If you spin the spinner to the right, what is the probability of spinning a:

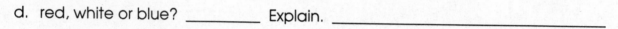

   a. blue? _____

   b. white? _____

   c. red? _____

   d. red, white or blue? _____ Explain. _____

   e. green? _____ Explain. _____

   f. What is the probability of not spinning a blue? _____ Explain. _____

   _____

9. Complete the following table and use it to answer the questions below.

   a. Find the probability of selecting

   an orange plain M&M _____

   a green M&M _____

   an orange peanut M&M _____

   a red M&M _____

   a yellow plain M&M _____

	Plain	Peanut	Total
red	7	8	
orange	5	0	
yellow	1	5	
lt brown	3	9	
dk brown	2	4	
green	6	7	
TOTAL			57

   b. Given that you pick a red M&M, what is the probability that it is plain? _____

   c. Given that you pick a dark brown M&M, what is the probability that it is peanut? _____

   d. Explain your answers. _____

   _____

   _____

A Coded Calendar

Name _____

OBJECTIVE: To use symbols and patterns to solve calendar puzzles

Use your current monthly calendar to create a coded approach to figuring out days and weeks.

ALL I CARE ABOUT IS **GAME DAY!!**

S	M	T	W	Th	F	S
1	2	3	4	5	6	7
8	9	10	11	12	13	14
15	16	17	18	19	20	21
22	23	24	25	26	27	28
29	30	31				

Use arrows to indicate changes in days or weeks.

→ is the next day	← was the day before
↓ is 1 week from today	↑ was one week ago today

Example:

23 → means the 24th

23 ↓ means the 30th

11 → ↓ → means the 20th

A. Complete the table using the above calendar.

	starting date/changes	new date
1.	1 ↓ → →	
2.	4 ← ↓ ↓ → →	
3.	13 ← ↑ → ↓	
4.	22 → → → ↑ → →	
5.	29 ↑ ↑ ↑ ↑ → → ↓ →	
6.	7 ← ↓ ← ↓ ← ↓	
7.	3 ↓ ↓ → → ↓ → ←	
8.	31 ↑ ← ↑ ↑ ← ↑	

B. Complete the table using the above calendar.

	starting date/changes	new date
1.	2	21
2.	26	30
3.	15	10
4.	7	25
5.	8	8
6.	11	27
7.	29	17
8.	12	23

43

Words Worth Money

OBJECTIVE: To use a coded alphabet to discover many "money" words

Codes can be a fun way to practice certain skills. In the activity below, each letter of the alphabet is worth a specific amount of money. The students try to find the most valuable words and sentences using the money alphabet. Give students a copy of the bottom of this page. Have them finish the chart. Then, put the following examples on the board and discuss them with the class.

Examples: Excellent is a $100 word.   Kristin is a $100 word.
Think of unusual situations:
Gold is worth $38, but silver is worth (<u>$85</u>)?
A dollar is really worth (<u>$62</u>)?

When students are familiar with the chart, ask them questions similar to the ones below. Then, have students finish the activity.

1. How many $100 words can you find? What are they?
2. How many $100 sentences can you find? What are they?
3. Change the pattern (i.e. even or odd amount increments). How many $150 or $200 words or sentences can you find?
4. Give students math sentences and ask them what the sentences are worth.

Words Worth Money

Name _____

1. How much is your name worth? _____

2. How much is your teacher's name worth? _____

3. What is your favorite sport? _____

   How much is it worth? _____

4. Name your brothers and sisters. _____

   _____

   How much are they worth? _____

   _____

5. How much is your school's name worth? _____

6. How much is your school mascot worth? _____

Letter	Worth	Letter	Worth
A	$1	N	
B	$2	O	
C		P	
D		Q	$17
E		R	
F		S	
G		T	
H		U	
I		V	$22
J		W	
K	$11	X	
L		Y	
M		Z	$26

44

Birthday Parties
(Math Without Numbers)

OBJECTIVE: To use matrix logic puzzles to organize thoughts and to approach problem solving in a more logical manner

Word-logic problems can be solved with little or no mathematical background. However, they do require/develop good reasoning skills. To work the problems, students should read the clues and make notes about the relationships between them. A matrix (table) is given for the students to fill in. This matrix will help students organize the information and allow for completion of the puzzle. You may want to help the students complete the puzzle below to help them learn how to use a matrix correctly.

Birthday Parties

Name _____

Directions:

During one week, there is a birthday party every day. No two children are invited to the same party. Find out the day that each child attends a party. (Start your matrix with Sunday and continue through Saturday.)

Clues:

1. Linda and Pat do not go to a party on a Friday or a Saturday.
2. Pat and Alex do not go on a Tuesday, but Susan does.
3. Jamie goes to a party on a Wednesday.
4. Jimmy goes to a party the day after Jamie.
5. Linda goes to a party the day before Pat.
6. Paul goes to a party on a Saturday.

Matrix:

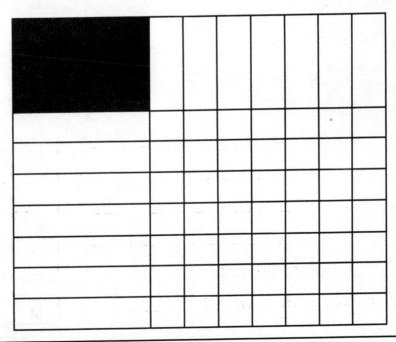

45

Shoes and Towels

Name _____

OBJECTIVE: To use matrix logic puzzles to organize thoughts and to approach problem solving in a more logical manner

In this word-logic problem, there are two items to keep track of for each boy. Using a process of elimination will be helpful! You may need to read the clues several times.

Directions:

Jeff, Ted, Steve and Chris all go to the beach. When they get out of the water, they notice that someone has mixed up their shoes and towels. Figure out which items belong to each of the boys.

Clues:

1. Steve's towel and shoes are the same color.
2. The person with the blue sneakers has a red towel.
3. One of the boys wears brown loafers.
4. Jeff has a green towel.
5. Jeff's shoes are the same color as Chris' towel.
6. If Chris' towel faded, it would be pink.
7. Ted has stitches in his big toe and cannot wear the red sandals.
8. Steve would rather go barefoot than wear the green running shoes.
9. Steve either has the blue or the brown towel.

Matrix:

	shoes blue	shoes red	shoes brown	shoes green	towel blue	towel red	towel brown	towel green
Steve	✓	✗	✗	✗	✓	✗	✗	✗
Chris	✓	✗	✗	✗	✗	✓	✗	✗
Ted	✗	✗	✗	✓	✗	✗	✓	✗
Jeff	✗	✓	✗	✗	✗	✗	✗	✓

Houses, Pets and Order

Name _____

OBJECTIVE: To use matrix logic puzzles to organize thoughts and to approach problem solving in a more logical manner

In this word-logic problem, there are three items to keep track of for each boy. Stay organized!

Directions:

Billy Brown, Willy White, Bobby Blue and George Green all live on the same street. Their houses are painted brown, white, blue and green; but no boy lives in a house that matches his last name. Each boy has a pet and its name does not begin with the same letter as its owner's name. Also, you must determine the location of each house. Is it first, second, third or fourth on the block?

Clues:

1. George owns the bear.
2. Willy owns the bull.
3. The white house is the last one on the street.
4. Neither the bear nor the bull live next to the first house.
5. Bobby's house is not green.
6. The boy who owns the whale lives in the green house.
7. The gorilla lives in the first house, which is brown.

Matrix:

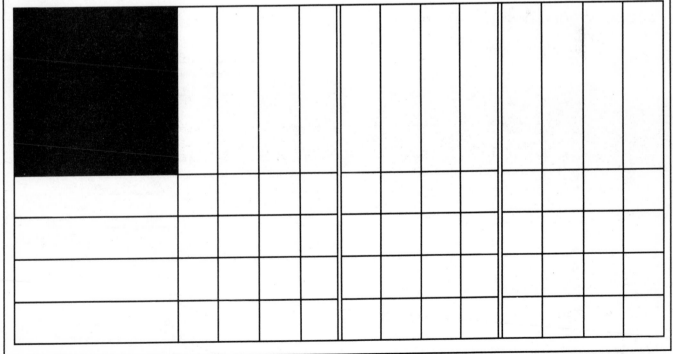

Make Your Own

Name _____

OBJECTIVE: To use matrix logic puzzles to organize thoughts and to approach problem solving in a more logical manner

Create your own word-logic problem! Try one with three people and two items to keep track of for each person.

Decide on your solution, then create some clues to give.

1. _____
2. _____
3. _____
4. _____
5. _____
5. _____
7. _____
8. _____

Use this puzzle to challenge a classmate. Can you create a more difficult or complex puzzle?

Company Communication

Name _____

OBJECTIVE: To use patterns and grouping to solve a friendly puzzle

On the map of the United States below, eleven cities are marked with dots. In each city is the office of a nationwide communication company with sales representatives who work with sales representatives in another city. The people who work together must get along. The eleven sales representatives are:

Annette	Elaine	Ira
Bill	Frank	James
Carl	Gail	Kim
David	Harold	

The friends are:

Annette and Bill	Frank and Harold	Ira and Kim
Ira and James	Gail and James	Gail and Ira
David and Elaine	James and Carl	David and Ira
Annette and Gail	Kim and Elaine	Kim and David
Carl and Harold	Annette and David	

Place the eleven sales representatives in the eleven cities so that they work with their friends in the connecting offices.

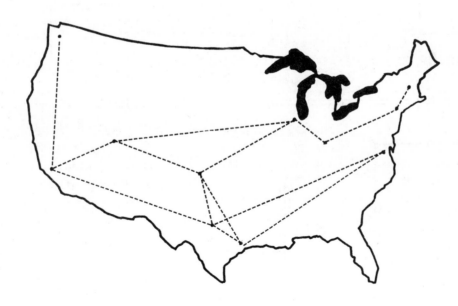

Sports Fever

Name _____

OBJECTIVE: To use "clues" to find the winners of four tournaments

A basketball league sets up a summer schedule with three mini-tournaments for the four teams in the league. The teams North, South, East and West each participate in the three tournaments that were set up in the manner below.

Given the following facts, complete each of the three tournament brackets.

1. South never defeated West.
2. North didn't win a single game.
3. West never defeated East.
4. Only North didn't win a championship.

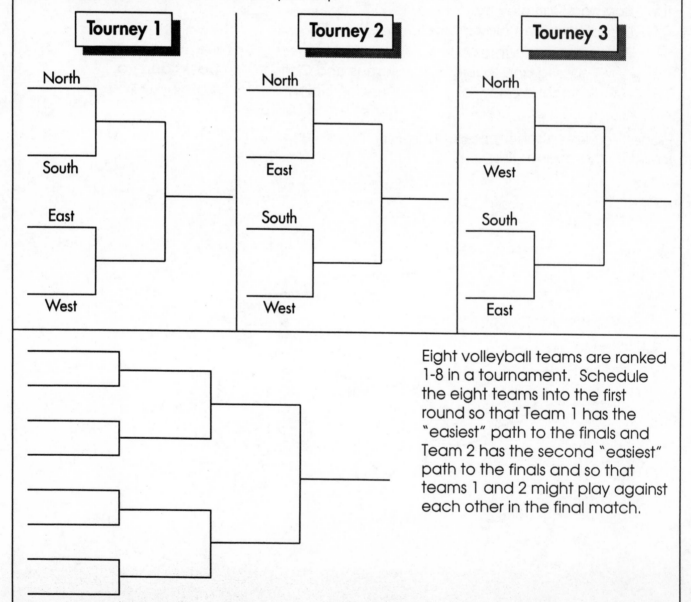

Eight volleyball teams are ranked 1-8 in a tournament. Schedule the eight teams into the first round so that Team 1 has the "easiest" path to the finals and Team 2 has the second "easiest" path to the finals and so that teams 1 and 2 might play against each other in the final match.

Meet the Players

Name _____

OBJECTIVE: To use several problem-solving strategies including organizing data and process of elimination to find out about players

The following five players play for the North team in the summer league. Get to know them and see if you can answer a few questions. The players are Al, Bob, Carl, David and Evan. Here are a few hints about them.

1. Two of them wear white shoes and three wear black shoes.
2. Al and David wear the same color of shoes.
3. Carl and Evan wear different colored shoes.
4. There are three forwards and two guards.
5. Bob and Carl play the same position.
6. David and Evan play different positions.
7. The guard who wears white shoes is the leading scorer on the team.

What position does each boy play and what color are his shoes?

	Position	Color of Shoes
Al	_____	_____
Bob	_____	_____
Carl	_____	_____
David	_____	_____
Evan	_____	_____

What is the leading scorer's name? _____

(Hint: Set up a matrix to help you organize your information.)

HEY- COOL SHOES!

GEE, THANKS!

Patterns I

OBJECTIVE: To explore patterns of numbers while working with perfect squares and sequences of numbers

Give students the following situation:

Eighteen players attended tryouts for the North team of the summer basketball league. They wore jerseys numbered 1-18. During the tryout, the coach ran them through a one-on-one shooting drill. During the drill, they happened to be paired up in such a way that each pair of players wore jersey numbers that added up to a perfect square. What were the numbers worn by the two players in each pair during this drill?

Pick one or all of the following activities to do to have the students answer the question.

1. Pick 18 students and pin a number from 1-18 on each of them. Have the remainder of students pair up the students with numbers on them in order to answer the question.

2. Put students in groups. Give each group index cards numbered 1-18. Have the groups race to answer the question.

3. Have students work individually with paper and pencil. They should race to answer the question. Let the three students who finish first discuss their strategy with the class.

4. Have students look at other number patterns and devise some cool problems.

Patterns II

Name _____

1. Find the next five terms for a-j. Write an expression to describe each pattern.

   a. 12, 18, 24, 30, ____ , ____ , ____ , ____ , ____

   b. 1, 2, 3, 5, 8, 13, 21, ____ , ____ , ____ , ____ , ____

   c. 75, 60, 45, ____ , ____ , ____ , ____ , ____

   d. 0.6, 3.6, 6.6, 9.6, ____ , ____ , ____ , ____ , ____

   e. 53, 50, 47, 44, ____ , ____ , ____ , ____ , ____

   f. 2, 12, 22, 32, ____ , ____ , ____ , ____ , ____

   g. 6.4, 8.2, 10, ____ , ____ , ____ , ____ , ____

   h. $1/4$, $1/2$, $3/4$, ____ , ____ , ____ , ____ , ____

   i. 17.9, 16.2, 14.5, ____ , ____ , ____ , ____ , ____

   j. 154, 166, 178, 190, ____ , ____ , ____ , ____ , ____

2. Write your own patterns. Write down three patterns (and how you formed them). Challenge a friend to figure out the next five terms and a possible expression to describe each pattern.

You Grade It! (A)

Name _____

OBJECTIVE: To find mistakes and correct them on a topics review guide

Find the mistakes on Susie's quiz below. When you find a mistake, circle the number of the problem and work it correctly in the space provided.

Problem	Answer	Corrections
1. $30 - 9 \times (2 + 1)$	3	
2. Find the value of $3n - 4$ if $n = 5$.	11	
3. Find the value of $a^2 + \frac{b}{3}$ if $a = 4, b = 2$.	$8\,^2/_3$	
4. Al has \$420 in his savings account. He deposits \$35. What is his new balance?	\$455	
5. $0.036 + 0.15 + 1.7$	1.886	
6. Subtract 1,661 from 23,208.	21,547	
7. A square with a side of 8' has a perimeter of __?	64'	
8. What are the missing pieces of this sequence: 9, 18, __, 36, __ ?	27, 45	
9. Find the average of 63, 47, 130.	80	
10. $\frac{7}{12} = \frac{x}{36}$	21	
11. Simplify $\frac{16}{18}$	$\frac{4}{9}$	
12. $5\frac{3}{4} + 11\frac{3}{4}$	$16\,^1/_2$	
13. $\frac{2}{3} \times \frac{1}{4}$	$\frac{1}{6}$	
14. $8 \div \frac{2}{3}$	12	
15. 28 kilograms = __ grams	28,000	
16. 67 inches = __ feet __ inches	5 ft 6 in.	
17. How much will it cost if a 4' x 6' area is carpeted at \$16.95 per square feet?	\$406.80	
18. What percent of 120 is 90?	75%	
19. 80 is what percent of 64?	80%	
20. $-18 - 5 = ?$	-23	

Just for Fun! (A)

Name _____

OBJECTIVE: To use various problem-solving skills to solve puzzling questions

1. Arrange the numbers 1 to 8 in the circles so that no two consecutive integers are in circles that are connected by line segments.

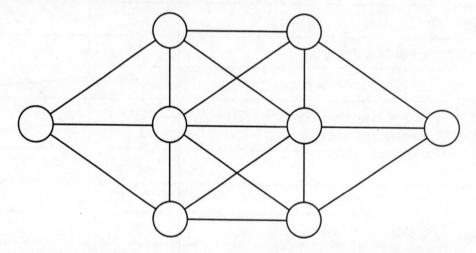

2. Draw two straight lines across the clock to divide it into three parts whose numbers within add up to 26.

3. Ms. Red, Ms. White and Ms. Blue were having lunch. One of them was wearing a red hat, one a white hat and one a blue hat. The lady wearing the blue hat said, "We are wearing hats that match our names, but not one of us is wearing a hat that matches the color of our name!" "What insight you have!" commented Ms. Red. What color hat was each lady wearing?

_____

54

Just for Fun! (A) continued

Name _____

4. Describe the pattern of the letters below. (Think numbers!)

_____

_____

OTTFFSSENT   FFFFFFFFFS

ETTFFSSENT   SSSSSSSSSS

TTTTTTTTTT   SSSSSSSSSE

TTTTTTTTTF   EEEEEEEEEN

FFFFFFFFFF   NNNNNNNNNO

5. A man offers to work for 30 days. He states his salary to be 1¢ the first day, 2¢ the second day, 4¢ the third day, etc. doubling his amount each day. Will he make too little or too much money for 30 days of work? _____

6. Substitute words for the numbers in this story by doing the math on your calculator and turning it upside-down to read the word.

(632 x 497) + 3433 and (2 x 5 x 7 x 110) + 18 went to the (677 + 271 − 946) ÷ 100. They walked up a (59,982 ÷ 13) (69,426 ÷ 9). (11,283 + 17,584) x 11 broke the (193 x 38) of her (1367 − 758) x 5 when (69 x 15) ÷ 3 stepped in a (49 x 56) + (12 x 80). (69 x 5) had to (66,666 + 77,777 + 88,888 + 99,999 + 45,474) around and her (91 x 7) hurt. (227 x 34) almost stepped on a (315,054 ÷ 9) (3 x 13 x 17).

7. Four friends stay at the same hotel for a wedding. Each person has a room on a different floor. Ally must ride the elevator down four floors to visit Ted. Bill is one floor below Kathy. Ted has a room on the tenth floor. Kathy must ride the elevator up six floors to visit Ally. Who is staying on which floor?

_____

_____

8. Ann, Bob and Carl have chosen careers as a teacher, a pediatrician and a lawyer. If Bob does not like to be around children and Ann cannot stand the sight of blood, who has chosen which career?

_____

Coordinate System Classroom (Quadrant 1)

OBJECTIVE: To physically become ordered pairs in the classroom in order to gain an understanding of the coordinate system and its ordered pairs

YOU WILL NEED:

- index cards

Turn your classroom into a coordinate system in Quadrant I. Give each student an index card as he/she enters the room. On one side of the card will be the basic instructions listed below. On the other side of the card will be an ordered pair. This will be the student's seating assignment for the day. Prior to the students' arrival, arrange your room into distinct rows and columns. For example:

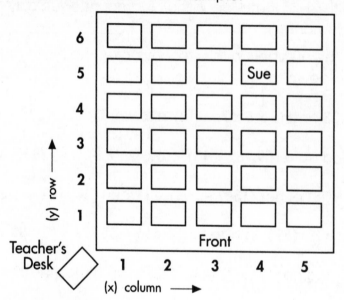

Sue has ordered pair (4, 5).

Make sure your ordered pairs "fit" your room arrangement.

Directions for each index card:

Begin at my desk. Move to the column number (the first number of the ordered pair). Then, move up the column to the row number (the second number of the ordered pair).

Double check each student's desk and ordered pair. Do activities with the students using this coordinate system. For example: Call a student up to the front of the room. Have him/her name a student who is seated. Have the standing student tell the ordered pair of the seated student. Repeat this process with other students and discuss how important an ordered pair is.

56

Coordinate System Classroom (All Four Quadrants)

YOU WILL NEED:
- index cards
- masking tape

OBJECTIVE: To physically become ordered pairs in the classroom in order to gain an understanding of the coordinate system and its ordered pairs

Turn your classroom into a coordinate system with four quadrants. Give each student an index card as he/she enters the room. On one side of the card will be the basic instructions listed below. On the other side of the card will be an ordered pair. This will be the student's seating assignment for the day. Prior to the students' arrival, arrange your room into distinct rows and columns and mark your floor with masking tape as shown.

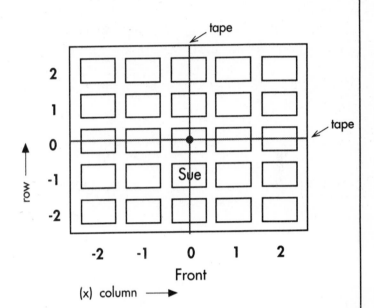

Sue has ordered pair (0, -1).

Directions for each index card:

Begin at (0, 0) (where the tape intersects) facing the back wall. Move the distance of your first number either right (+) or left (–). Then, move the distance of your second number either forward (+) or backward (–).

Double check each student's desk and ordered pair. Do activities with the students using this coordinate system. For example: Call a student up to the front of the room. Have him/her name a student who is seated. Have the standing student tell the ordered pair of the seated student. Repeat this process with other students. Another example is to have all students from Quadrant I stand. Discuss the coordinate system. Discuss points that lie on the axis, etc.

Map Reading

Name _____

OBJECTIVE: To make comparisons between maps and coordinate systems in order to understand the relationship of ordered pairs and grids

Use the map to the right to answer the questions below.

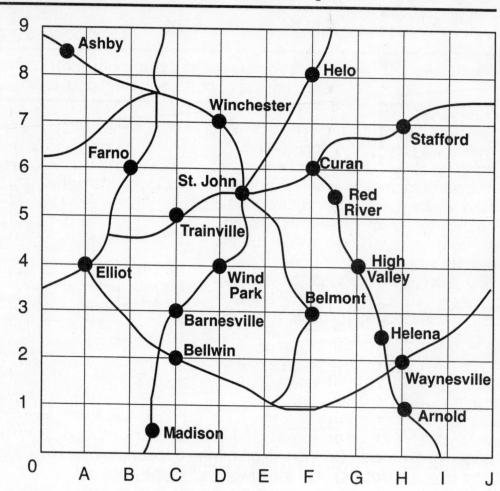

Use an ordered pair (a letter and a number) to give the location of the following towns.

1. Arnold _____
2. Winchester _____
3. Stafford _____

4. Wind Park _____
5. Belmont _____
6. Trainville _____

Name the town located at each point.

7. (C, 2) _____
8. (A, 4) _____
9. (G, 4) _____

10. (B, 6) _____
11. (H, 2) _____
12. (F, 6) _____

Battleship (Instructions/Example)

OBJECTIVE: To play the game of battleship while practicing ordered pairs, coordinate systems and problem-solving skills

Pair up students. Have the pairs turn their desks to face each other. Each student should use a book as a game holder. (Have students open the cover to create a private table.) Give each student a copy of page 60 "Battleship A." Each student has five ships—a one-man, a two-man, a three-man, a four-man and a five-man ship. Ships can be placed vertically, horizontally or diagonally as long as each "man" is on a point on the grid. Students should put their ships on the upper "My Ship" grid on the page. After both players have hidden their ships in the upper grid, the game can begin. The rules for the game need to be understood by all players before beginning.

Rules:

The youngest of the pair is Player One. To begin, Player One gets five guesses to try to find Player B's ships. After all five guesses, Player Two must tell which guesses were hits and which ship(s) was sunk. Then, Player Two gets five guesses and Player One must tell which were hit and sunk. The play continues alternating turns. The only catch is that when one player loses a ship, he/she loses a guess (i.e. If Player Two only has three ships left, he/she only gets three guesses instead of five.). A player wins when he/she sinks all five of the opponent's ships.

Tell students that an easy way to keep track of what they call is to make marks on their grids. For example: On the top grid, if the opposing player hits a ship, tell students to put an x over the dot (✗). On the lower grid, as they call out ordered pairs, they should make a dot on the points called. If the dot was a hit, have them cross it out (✗). This way students won't call the same points over and over and waste guesses.

To give students practice using all four quadrants, give them page 61, "Battleship B."

Player One

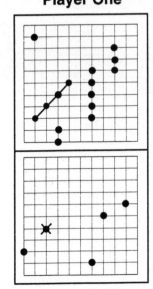

Example

1. Player One places his/her ships as shown.

2. Player One guesses (2, 4), (6, 1), (9, 6), (7, 5) and (0, 2).

3. Player Two tells him/her that (2, 4) is a hit on the two-man ship. (Player Two still has five guesses because his/her two-man ship was hit but not sunk.)

Battleship A

Name _____

My Ships

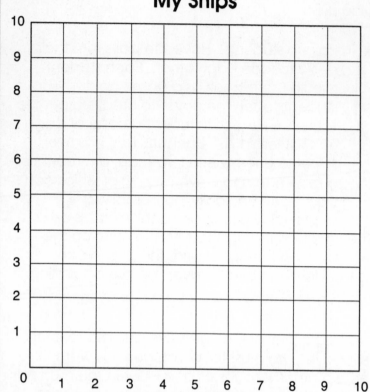

Ships:

Enemy Ships

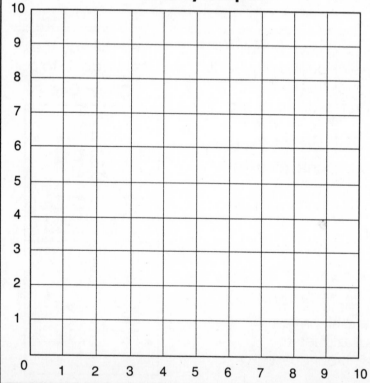

Location:

• ( )

•• ( )( )

••• ( )( )( )

•••• ( )( )( )
( )

••••• ( )( )( )
( )( )

60

Battleship B

Name _____

My Ships

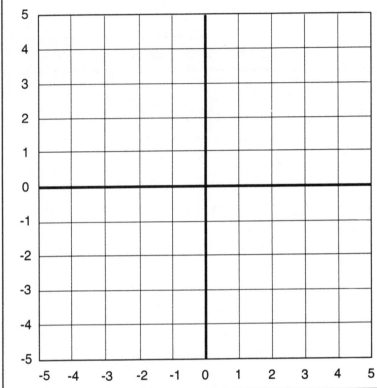

Ships:

●

● ●

● ● ●

● ● ● ●

● ● ● ● ●

Enemy Ships

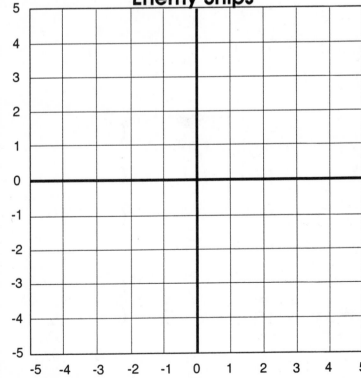

Location:

●　　(　)

● ●　　(　)(　)

● ● ●　　(　)(　)(　)

● ● ● ●　　(　)(　)(　)
　　　　　(　)

● ● ● ● ●　　(　)(　)(　)
　　　　　(　)(　)

Pictures

YOU WILL NEED:

graph paper

OBJECTIVE: To create pictures by organizing ordered pairs on a grid

Ordered pairs can be used to create pictures. Try one or all of the following activities to let your students become experts at ordered pairs.

A. Have students draw and connect the following points (in order) to create a design. Ask students what they created. (star)

(1, 1), (6, 4), (11, 1), (8, 5), (11, 8), (7, 8), (6, 11), (5, 8), (1, 8), (4, 5), (1, 1)

B. Have your students draw a house (or other object) on a grid and group the points in order of connecting. Put the following example on the overhead so students can complete it. The main frame of the house is section A, the door is section B, and a window is section C.

Section A = (5, 1), (5, 8), (8, 12), (11, 8), (11, 1), (5, 1)

Section B = (7, 1), (7, 4), (9, 4), (9, 1)

Section C = (8, 5), (8, 7), (10, 7), (10, 5), (8, 5)

Encourage students to be creative and add several windows, chimneys, etc.

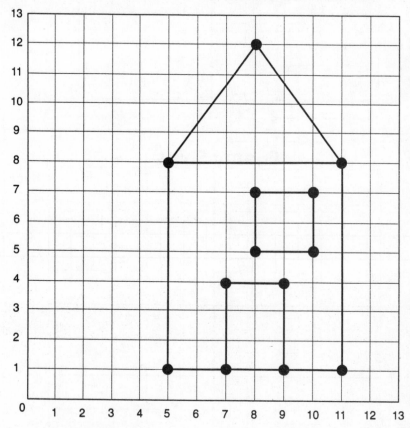

C. Have students make a design on a grid. Then, on another sheet of paper, have the students write the ordered pairs. Tell students that to begin another section, they should label each section or write, "Lift pencil." Collect the ordered pairs and pass them out making sure no one gets his/her own back. Have students create each other's designs.

Just for Fun! (B)

Name _____

OBJECTIVE: To find area using a grid

YOU FOLKS HAVE BEEN GREAT... GIVE YOUR-SELVES A BIG HAND!

Estimate the area of your hand in square inches. Then, outline your hand on the grid below. Separate the outline of your hand into regular and irregular shapes. (Using the squares on the grid as regular.) Calculate as best you can the actual area of your hand based on the grid measurements. Compare your original estimate and your calculated results. How close were you? Try to estimate other objects in your classroom using this same procedure.

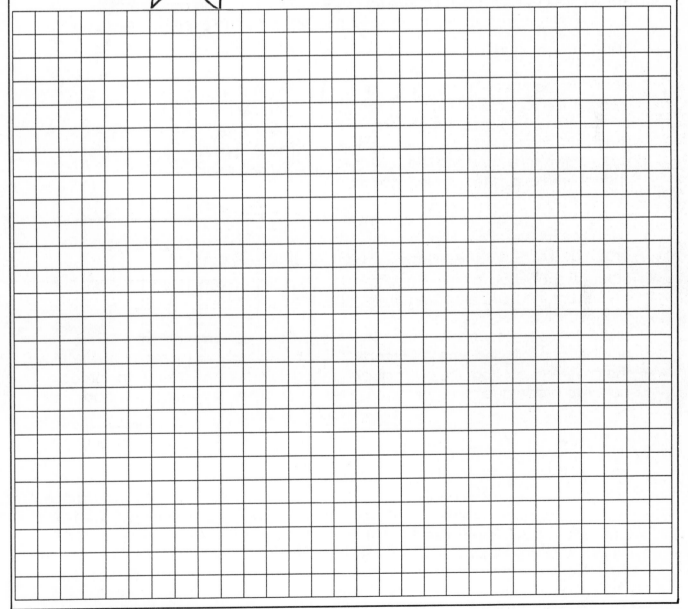

Heart to Heart

OBJECTIVES: To gather data, organize it, analyze it, and then graph it; To make comparisons and draw relationships using the information gathered

One of the most useful applications of a graph is to compare two situations on the same graph. In this activity, students will measure and record their heartbeats in a relaxed state. Then, students measure and record their heartbeats after exercising. Both measurements will be recorded on the same graph so that an easy comparison can be made. This activity should generate discussion about how ordered pairs are formed and used to graph lines, etc. Some questions to ask students when the graphs are complete are, "Why are the measurements different along the axes? How do the graphs differ? From the graph, can you describe what happens to the heart rate after exercising?"

Directions

A. Give each student a copy of page 65. Each student should find his/her pulse (on wrist or neck). Students should count the number of times their heart beats in ten seconds and record that information. (You should keep time for the students.) Have students repeat this process five times and find the average. The table relating the number of beats and time in seconds on page 65 should then be completed by the students.

DUUUUDE, WHAT IF, LIKE, YOU KNOW, YOU CAN'T LIKE, Y'KNOW, FIND A PULSE OR NOTHIN'?

Using the ordered pairs from this data, students should use a colored pencil to graph and connect the ordered pairs on the graph on page 66.

B. Students should jog in place for 30 seconds and then immediately find their pulse and count the number of times their heart beats in ten seconds. The information should then be recorded on the page. This process should be repeated by the students five times, and the average should be found. The table relating the number of beats and time in seconds should be completed by the students. Using the ordered pairs from this data, students should then use a different-colored pencil to graph and connect the ordered pairs on the same graph on page 66.

JOG?! DUUUDE, YOU MEAN, LIKE, EXERCISE?

C. Give students another copy of page 66. This time, students should make a bar graph showing both sets of data. On their own paper, students should then write in report (paragraph) form the purpose of their "experiment," how the data was gathered, how it was organized, what mathematical models were used to analyze it and what it all means. Then, they should describe a different project they could do using the same pattern for making comparisons and identifying relationships.

64

Heart to Heart

Name _____

OBJECTIVES: To gather data and organize, analyze, and graph it; To make comparisons and draw conclusions using the information gathered

A. Trial 1 _____ beats per ten seconds

Trial 2 _____ beats per ten seconds

Trial 3 _____ beats per ten seconds

Trial 4 _____ beats per ten seconds

Trial 5 _____ beats per ten seconds

(add number of beats and divide by five) = average beats per ten seconds ☐

(Round to the nearest whole number.)

time in seconds (t)	10	20	30	40	50	60
number of beats (b)						

Assume that the number of beats in 20 seconds would be twice that in ten seconds, etc.

State the ordered pairs from the table (t, b).

(10,) (   ) (   ) (   ) (   ) (   ) (   )

B. Trial 1 _____ beats per ten seconds

Trial 2 _____ beats per ten seconds

Trial 3 _____ beats per ten seconds

Trial 4 _____ beats per ten seconds

Trial 5 _____ beats per ten seconds

(add number of beats and divide by five) = average beats per ten seconds ☐

(Round to the nearest whole number.)

time in seconds (t)	10	20	30	40	50	60
number of beats (b)						

Assume that the number of beats in 20 seconds would be twice that in ten seconds, etc.

State the ordered pairs from the table (t, b).

(10,) (   ) (   ) (   ) (   ) (   ) (   )

Heart to Heart

Name _____

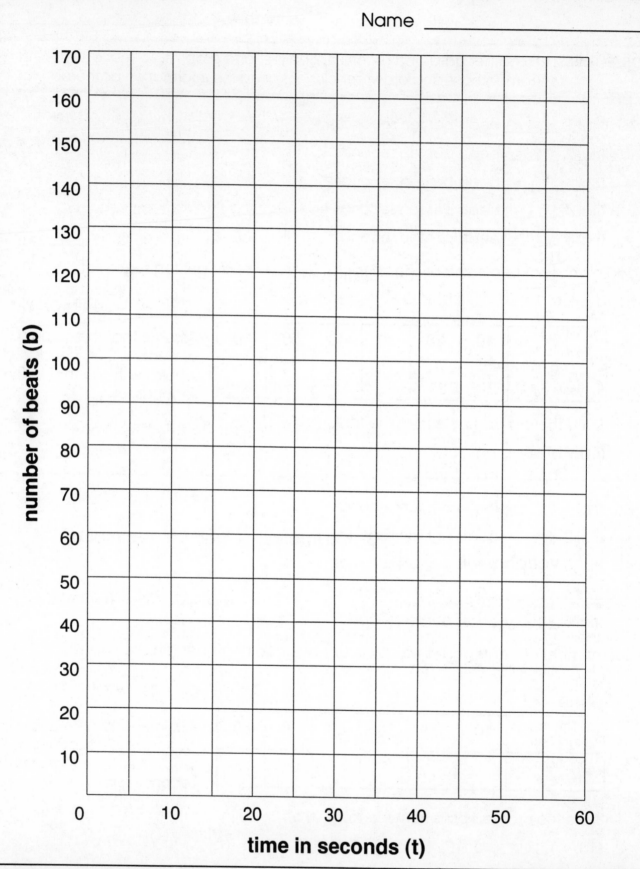

number of beats (b)

time in seconds (t)

66

Equation-Solving Skills

Name _____

OBJECTIVE: To follow a flow chart to recognize the order and patterns of equation solving

Use the flow chart below to help "put it all together" when learning about equation solving.

1. **Is it a subtraction problem?**
   - no
   - yes → **Change it to an addition sentence.**

2. **Are there grouping symbols?**
   - no
   - yes → **Distribute.**

3. **Are there variables on the right side?**
   - no
   - yes → **Move them to the left side.**

   combine/simplify left side

4. **Is there a number *not* attached to the variable?**
   - no
   - yes → **Move it to the right side (combine).**

5. **Is there a number attached to the variable?**
   - no
   - yes →
     1. if by ⊗ → then ÷
     2. if by ÷ → then ⊗
     3. if a fraction → then use reciprocal

   variable = #

   variable = #

Solve these problems using the flow chart above.

1. $y + 7 = 5$

2. $-8 + x = -12$

3. $-2 = a - 17$

4. $4x = -16$

5. $-18y = -9$

6. $\frac{-3}{2}x = 6$

7. $4(n + 2) = -20$

8. $-15 = 2(x + 3)$

9. $3x - 2 = -11$

10. $2y + 7 = -42$

11. $3(x + 2) = 5x + 10$

12. $-4x + 2(x + 1) = 7x - 16$

Make a Table/Draw a Picture (Distance)

Name _____

OBJECTIVES: To use pictures, diagrams and tables to organize the information from word problems; To write and solve algebraic equations relating to the tables to answer the questions

Often when solving a math word problem, it is helpful to make a table to help you organize the information from the problem. The two most common uses of a table are for distance and mixture problems.

Distance Problem Example

recall that distance = rate times time—$D = r \times t$

Two motorcycles 635 miles apart start at the same time and travel toward each other. Motorcycle Mike travels at a rate of 52 miles per hour and Motorcycle Matt travels at a rate of 75 miles per hour. In how many hours will they meet?

A. Fill in the given information and represent the unknown with a variable.

	r	t	D
Mike	52	t	52t
Matt	75	t	75t

B. Use a picture or diagram to help you "see" what is occurring in the problem.

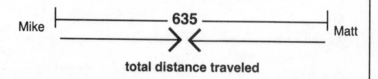

total distance traveled

C. Write the equation—the distance Mike travels plus the distance Matt travels equals 635 miles. Then, solve the equation.

Fill in the equation:

Answer: The time each man travels is ____ hours. Therefore, they will meet in ____ hours.

Make a Table/Draw a Picture (Mixture)

Name _____

OBJECTIVES: To use pictures, diagrams and tables to organize the information from word problems; To write and solve algebraic equations relating to the tables to answer the questions

Mixture Problem Example

Cathy's Candy Store wants to mix plain M&M's that sell for $4.00 per kilogram with peanuts that sell for $5.75 per kilogram to make a 100 kilogram mixture that sells for $4.70 per kilogram. How many kilograms of M&M's and peanuts must be used?

A. Fill in the given information and represent the unknown with a variable. If the total kilograms equals 100, then M&M's plus peanuts must equal 100. Solve for one or the other.

	# of kilo	Price	Total Value
M&M's	x	$4.00	4.00 (x)
peanuts	100 – x	$5.75	5.75 (100 – x)
mixture	100	$4.70	4.70 (100)

B. Write a sentence to describe what is occurring in the problem.

$\boxed{\text{M&M's}}$ + $\boxed{\text{Peanuts}}$ =

total value of M&M's + total value of peanuts

= total value of mixture

$\boxed{\text{Mixture}}$

C. Write an equation using the information in the last column of the table. Then, solve the equation for both x and 100 – x.

Fill in the equation.

Answer: _____ kilograms of M&M's and _____ kilograms of peanuts will be needed for the desired mixture.

Make a Table/Draw a Picture (Distance and Mixture)

Name _____

OBJECTIVES: To use pictures, diagrams and tables to organize the information from word problems; To write and solve equations relating to the tables to answer the questions

For each problem, make a table and draw a picture or write a statement describing what is occurring. Then, set up an equation and solve. Be sure to answer the question completely.

1. Two bicyclists start at the same time from the same place and travel in opposite directions. One travels 45 miles per hour, the other 40 miles per hour. In how many hours will they be 255 miles apart?

2. How many kilograms of Coffee A selling at $6.00 per kilogram must be mixed with 20 kilograms of Coffee B selling at $3.25 per kilogram to get a mixture worth $4.50 a kilogram?

3. A 25% gold alloy is melted to a 55% gold alloy. How many grams of each must be used to obtain 30 grams of a 32% gold alloy?

4. Two airplanes leave St. Louis at the same time. The rate of the second plane (flying north) is 100 kilometers per hour faster than the first (flying south). In three hours, they are 4800 kilometers apart. Find each airplane's rate.

5. Bob has a mixture of dimes and nickels worth $5.00. He has 66 coins total. How many of each coin does he have?

Algebraic Geometry

OBJECTIVE: To draw and label geometric shapes to visualize and solve word problems

Many geometry problems can be solved using algebra skills. Since shapes are involved, it is most often helpful to draw a picture, then "define the variable" and solve.

Example: The length of a rectangle is 7 inches longer than the width.
The perimeter is 54 inches. Find the length and width.

A. Draw a rectangle. Assign variables from the statement.

x = width

$x + 7$ = length

$x + 7$

x

B. perimeter = $2(l) + 2(w)$
Plug in your variables.

$2(x + 7) + 2(x) = 54$

C. Solve the equation and answer the statement completely.

$2x + 14 + 2x = 54$
$4x = 40$
$x = 10$
$x + 7 = 17$

Answer:
width = 10 inches
length = 17 inches

Make a copy of the bottom of this page for every student. After you go over the example above, have the students complete the problem below following the same steps. Then, go over the answer as a class.

Some students may need more practice to really grasp this process. After students are familiar with solving these types of problems, give them a copy of page 72. Have students work individually to solve the problems. Make sure students show all of the steps.

- -

Problem:

Name _____

The length of a rectangle is 3 times the width.
The perimeter is 120 meters. Find the length and the width.

A. Draw a picture and assign variables.

B. Write equation.

C. Solve equation.

$3x$

x

x = width
$3x$ = length

Answer: width = _____ meters

length = _____ meters

Algebraic Geometry

Name _____

OBJECTIVE: To draw and label geometric shapes to visualize and solve word problems

---

Solve each problem by drawing a picture, defining the variables, writing an equation and solving.

---

1. The length of a rectangle is 4 inches more than the width. The perimeter is 40 kilometers. Find the length and the width.

---

2. The perimeter of a rectangle is 82 feet. The length is 5 feet more than twice the width. Find the length and the width.

---

3. A rectangular field has a perimeter of 174 meters. The length of the field is 9 meters more than twice the width. Find the dimensions of the field.

---

4. The perimeter of a triangle is 37 centimeters. Two sides of the triangle are equal; each of these is 5 cm more than the third side. Find the length of each of the three sides.

---

5. Side A of a triangle is 3 inches longer than side B. Side C is one inch shorter than twice side B. The perimeter of the triangle is 26 inches. Find the length of each of the three sides.

---

6. A 33 kilometer bicycle race course is designed in the shape of a triangle. The first leg of the race is 5 km shorter than the second, and the third leg is twice the first. Find the distance of each leg of the race.

Algebra

Think About This...

Name _____

OBJECTIVE: To solve word problems

Solve each problem below.

---

1. An odd number is greater than 7 x 3 and less than 9 x 4. Find the number if the sum of its digits is 11.

---

2. Bob has three fewer nickels than dimes, and two more dimes than quarters. How much money does he have if he has three quarters?

---

3. A clock strikes the number of hours each hour. How many times will the clock strike in a 24-hour day?

---

4. Mr. Math is decorating his rectangular bulletin board. He is using black and red strips to border it. The width, which will be black, is 11 feet. The height, which will be red, is 6 feet. How many feet of each color ribbon does he need?

---

5. A square, a triangle and a circle are each a different color. The figure that is round is not green, one of the figures is red, and the blue figure has four equal sides. Find the color of each figure.

---

6. Billy picked a number between 1 and 10. If he adds 6, subtracts 8, then adds 9, the result is 12. What number did Billy pick?

---

7. Using each of the numbers 1, 2, 3 and 4 only once, find two 2-digit numbers that will give the greatest possible product when multiplied.

---

8. In a farmyard containing chickens and pigs, there are 54 heads and 144 feet. How many chickens are in the farmyard? How many pigs?

73

You Grade It! (B)

Algebra

Name _____

OBJECTIVE: To find mistakes and correct them on a topics review guide

Find the mistakes on Tom's quiz below. When you find a mistake, circle the number of the problem and work it correctly in the space provided.

Problem	Answer	Corrections
1. A rectangular stadium has a perimeter of 3,270 m. One side measures 545 m. What are the lengths of the other sides?	545 1090 1090	
2. It will cost the Student Council $300 for a disc jockey, $125 for room rental, $85 for decorations and $65 for refreshments for the Fall Dance. a. How much money does the Student Council need to sponsor the dance?	a. $575	
b. If they expect 300 students to attend and wish to make a minimum of $400 in profits, how much should they charge each student?	b. $3.00	
3. The "Raiders" (a little league team), is going to a St. Louis Cardinals baseball game. Each athlete is allowed to buy a hot dog ($3.25), a soda pop ($1.75) and peanuts ($1.25). If 17 athletes are going to the game, how much money is needed to buy each athlete all three items?	$106.25	
4. On the average, 12 of the 30 days in June in St. Louis are rainy. What fraction, in simplest form, of the days in June are <u>not</u> rainy?	$\frac{2}{5}$	
5. Bill ran a marathon in 3 hr 48 min 10 sec. Boyd ran it in 4 hr 27 min 35 sec. How much faster than Boyd was Bill?	1 hr 39 min 25 sec	

page 6—Wallpaper It Right!

1. a. $14' \times 8' = 112'$

   $10' \times 8' = 80'$

   $\underline{-16'}$ (minus 4' x 4' window)

   $64'$

   $14' \times 8' = 112'$

   $10' \times 8' = 80'$ (minus 5' x 6' closet

   $-30'$ and 3' x 7' door)

   $\underline{-21'}$

   $29'$

   $\underline{\qquad\qquad}$

   317 **square feet**

   b. $\frac{317}{28} = 11.3$ (Need 12 rolls.)

   c. $191.76

2. a. $14 + 10 + 14 + 10 = 48$ feet of border

   b. 48 feet = 16 yards

   $\frac{16}{5} = 3.2$ (Need 4 rolls.)

   c. $59.96

3. $191.76 + $59.96 = $251.72

pages 7-10—Metric Comparisons

I.		II.		III.	
1.	b	1.	b	1.	mL
2.	c	2.	a	2.	L
3.	a	3.	c	3.	L
4.	a	4.	b	4.	kL
5.	b	5.	c	5.	mL

pages 11-13—You Write the Properties

#1	Commutative for Addition	$a + b = b + a$	(Order won't affect sum.)
#2	Associative for Addition	$a + (b + c) = (a + b) + c$	(Grouping won't affect sum.)
#3	Additive Identity	$a + 0 = 0 + a = a$	(Adding zero won't change number.)
#4	Commutative for Multiplication	$a \bullet b = b \bullet a$	(Order won't affect product.)
#5	Associative for Multiplication	$a(bc) = (ab)c$	(Grouping won't affect product.)
#6	Multiplicative Identity	$a \bullet 1 = 1 \bullet a = a$	(Multiplying by 1 won't change number.)
#7	Distributive	$a(b + c) = ab + ac$	(Can write product as a sum.)

page 16—Making Change

	5¢	10¢	25¢	50¢		5¢	10¢	25¢	50¢
1.	—	—	—	2	21.	8	1	2	—
2.	—	—	2	1	22.	6	2	2	—
3.	1	2	1	1	23.	4	3	2	—
4.	—	5	—	1	24.	2	4	2	—
5.	2	4	—	1	25.	—	5	2	—
6.	4	3	—	1	26.	5	—	3	—
7.	6	2	—	1	27.	3	1	3	—
8.	8	1	—	1	28.	1	2	3	—
9.	10	—	—	1	29.	—	—	4	—
10.	3	1	1	1	30.	—	10	—	—
11.	5	—	1	1	31.	2	9	—	—
12.	15	—	1	—	32.	4	8	—	—
13.	13	1	1	—	33.	6	7	—	—
14.	11	2	1	—	34.	8	6	—	—
15.	9	3	1	—	35.	10	5	—	—
16.	7	4	1	—	36.	12	4	—	—
17.	5	5	1	—	37.	14	3	—	—
18.	3	6	1	—	38.	16	2	—	—
19.	1	7	1	—	39.	18	1	—	—
20.	10	—	2	—	40.	20	—	—	—

pages 17-19—
The Answer Is the Problem

+ and −

1. $15 - 3 - 12$
2. $15 - 12 + 5$
3. $12 + 5 - 15$
4. $12 + 5 + 3$
5. $15 - 5 - 3$
6. $15 + 3 - 5$

All 4 Operations

1. $2 \times 3 + 6$
2. $2 \times 4 - 3$
3. $4 + 2 \times 3$
4. $6 \times 4 + 3$
5. $3 \times 6 - 4$
6. $2 \times 6 + 3$

Fractions

1. $\frac{7}{12} - \frac{1}{12}$
2. $\frac{7}{12} + \frac{5}{12}$
3. $\frac{7}{12} - \frac{5}{12}$
4. $\frac{7}{12} + \frac{11}{12}$
5. $\frac{5}{12} - \frac{1}{12}$
6. $\frac{7}{12} + \frac{1}{12}$

Challenge $\frac{7}{12} + \frac{5}{12} - \frac{1}{12} - \frac{11}{12}$

page 20—
The Answer Is the Puzzle

```
10 - 4 - 4 = 2
 -     +   +
 2 + 8 + 1 = 11
 -     -   -
 7 + 2 + 3 = 12
 =     =   =
 1    10   2
```

```
7 + 4 - 6 = 5
+     +   +
6 + 7 - 5 = 8
-     -   -
5 + 3 - 8 = 0
=     =   =
8     8   3
```

Answer Key

page 21—The Answer Is the Puzzle

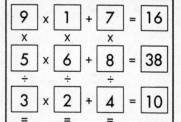

9	x	1	+	7	=	16
x		x		x		
5	x	6	+	8	=	38
÷		÷		÷		
3	x	2	+	4	=	10
=		=		=		
15		3		14		

5	x	4	÷	2	=	10
x		+		+		
6	x	9	÷	3	=	18
÷		−		+		
5	+	7	−	8	=	4
=		=		=		
6		6		13		

pages 23-24—Tangrams

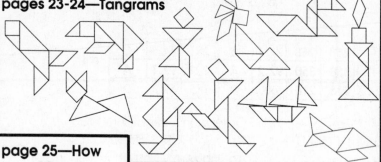

page 25—How Many?

1.
2. 27 triangles
3. 13 squares
4. 77 cards

pages 26-27—1 Is to 2 as 3 Is to ?

A.
1. A   5. ⊙
2. E
3. A   6. ◧
4. C

B.
1. C   5. ⊢
2. D
3. D   6. ◖
4. B

page 22—Golf Field Trip

SCORE CARD

HOLE	YARDS	SCORE
1	210	2
2	240	2
3	180	2
4	120	2
5	360	3
6	330	3
7	300	2
8	270	3
9	420	4
TOTAL SCORE		**23**

one of each—coffee mug, T-shirt, sweatshirt, shorts, poster, raincoat

pages 28-29—Box It Up

A.
C	C	C	D	D
G	G	C	D	D
B	A	A	F	F
B	B	A	A	F
B	H	E	E	E

B.
E	H	A	B	C	C
E	A	A	B	B	C
E	A	G	B	I	C
D	D	G	F	I	I
D	D	F	F	I	I

page 31—Teacher for the Day (Class Summary)

1. See gradebook
2.

	# of students	% of class
A	7	35%
B	5	25%
C	3	15%
D	4	20%
F	1	5%
	20	

3.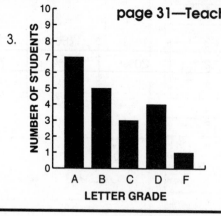

4.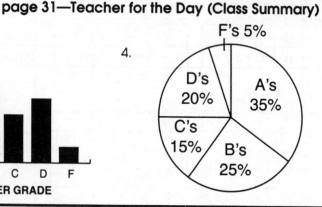

F's 5%, D's 20%, A's 35%, C's 15%, B's 25%

5. a. $\frac{1617}{20}$ = 80.9%,
   b. Gail had an 81

6. Steve stayed the same 61.9%. Paul raised his 58.1% to a 60% D. Kevin lowered his 64.5% to a 59.4% F.

7. a. See gradebook (last 2 columns).

b. none
c. Sue, John, Sam, Kristin, Stacy
d. Jim, Bob, Gail, Pam, Cathy, Earl, Jane, Julie, Paul, Scott, Carly, Jack
e. Steve, Kevin, Molly

page 33—Teacher for the Day (Specifics)

1. Steve 61.9%, Paul 58.1%, Kevin 64.5%
2. a. $\frac{869}{20}$ = 43.5 points
   b. Molly, 55, 100%
   c. Paul, 24, 43.6%
3. a. $\frac{490}{20}$ = 24.5 points

= 81.7%, B
   b. Jim, Jane
4. a. $\frac{2559}{20}$ = 128.0
   b. Molly, 154, 99.4%, yes
   c. Paul, 90, 58.1%, yes

page 32—Teacher for the Day (Grade Book)

Cumulative Possible Points	wk 1	55	wk 2	155	wk 3	240	wk 4	360	Total	%	Grade	Adjusted Total	Adjusted %	Adjusted Grade
Sue	49	49	85	134	70	204	96	300	300	83.3	B	260	83.9	B
Jim	44	44	76	120	69	189	89	278	278	77.2	C	235	75.8	C
Bob	53	53	96	149	81	230	118	348	348	96.7	A	299	96.5	A
Gail	41	41	84	125	73	198	97	295	295	81.9	B	249	80.3	B
Steve	31	31	65	96	52	148	75	223	223	61.9	D	192	61.9	D
Pam	46	46	90	136	72	208	105	313	313	86.9	B	268	86.5	B
Cathy	50	50	98	148	81	229	113	342	342	95	A	292	94.2	A
Earl	38	38	85	123	65	188	95	283	283	78.6	C	241	77.7	C
John	49	49	95	144	71	215	112	327	327	90.8	A	288	92.9	A
Jane	43	43	87	130	80	210	106	316	316	87.8	B	268	86.5	B
Sam	37	37	76	113	64	177	91	268	268	74.4	C	231	74.5	C
Julie	55	55	97	152	81	233	117	350	350	97.2	A	301	97.1	A
Paul	24	24	66	90	52	142	74	216	216	60	D	185	59.7	D
Scott	35	35	76	111	62	173	66	239	239	66.4	D	201	64.8	D
Carly	37	37	75	112	62	174	75	249	249	69.2	D	210	67.7	D
Kevin	32	32	68	100	50	150	64	214	214	59.4	F	184	59.4	F
Kristin	53	53	94	147	76	223	115	338	338	93.9	A	292	94.2	A
Jack	49	49	89	138	79	217	110	327	327	90.8	A	278	89.7	A
Stacy	48	48	89	137	70	207	102	309	309	85.8	B	270	87.1	B
Molly	55	55	99	154	85	239	122	361	361	100+	A	311	100+	A

page 34—Teacher for the Day (Battle of the Sexes)

1.

	total #	# of girls	# of boys	% of class	% of % girls	% of % boys
A	7	4	3	35%	57%	43%
B	5	5	0	25%	100%	0%
C	3	0	3	15%	0%	100%
D	4	1	3	20%	25%	75%
F	1	0	1	5%	0%	100%
	20	10	10			

2.

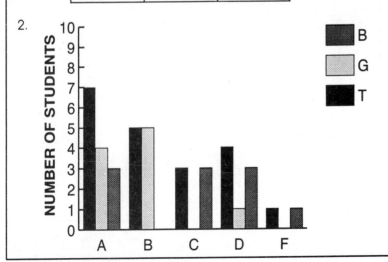

3.

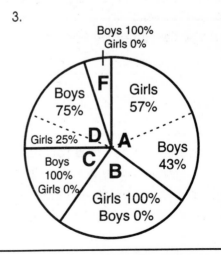

Answer Key

page 36—Basic Counting Principle

1. business trip: $2 \times 3 \times 2 = 12$

   $S^1T^1H^1$, $S^1T^1H^2$, $S^1T^2H^1$, $S^1T^2H^2$, $S^1T^3H^1$, $S^1T^3H^2$, $S^2T^1H^1$, $S^2T^1H^2$, $S^2T^2H^1$, $S^2T^2H^2$, $S^2T^3H^1$, $S^2T^3H^2$

2. sundae: $2 \times 2 \times 2 = 8$ CCP, CCW, CFP, CFW, VCP, VCW, VFP, VFW

pages 41 and 42—Probability (What Have You Learned?)

1. $3 \times 2 \times 3 = 18$

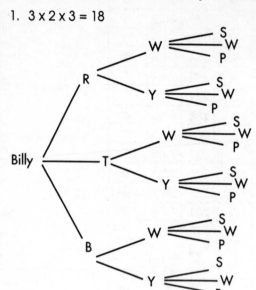

RWS
RWW
RWP
RYS
RYW
RYP
TWS
TWW
TWP
TYS
TYW
TYP
BWS
BWW
BWP
BYS
BYW
BYP

2. $^1/_2$

3. $^1/_4$ ($^1/_2 \times {}^1/_2$)

4. $^1/_6$

5. $^1/_{36}$ ($^1/_2 \times {}^1/_2$)

6. a. $^1/_4$

   b. $^1/_2$

   c. $^1/_4$

7. $^1/_4$ ($^4/_{16}$ reduced)

8. a. $^1/_4$ d. 1

   b. $^1/_4$ e. 0

   c. $^1/_2$ f. $^3/_4$

9. a. $^5/_{57}$, $^{13}/_{57}$, 0, $^{15}/_{57}$, $^1/_{57}$

   b. $^7/_{15}$

   c. $^2/_3$

	Plain	Peanut	Total
red	7	8	15
orange	5	0	5
yellow	1	5	6
lt brown	3	9	12
dk brown	2	4	6
green	6	7	13
TOTAL	24	33	57

page 43—A Coded Calendar

A. 1. 10   4. 20   7. 26   B. Answers
   2. 19   5. 11   8. 1   will vary.
   3. 13   6. 25

page 44—Words Worth Money

Letter	A	B	C	D	E	F	G	H	I	J	K	L	M
Worth	$1	$2	$3	$4	$5	$6	$7	$8	$9	$10	$11	$12	$13
Letter	N	O	P	Q	R	S	T	U	V	W	X	Y	Z
Worth	$14	$15	$16	$17	$18	$19	$20	$21	$22	$23	$24	$25	$26

page 45—Birthday Parties

Linda—Sunday   Jimmy—Thursday
Pat—Monday   Alex—Friday
Susan—Tuesday   Paul—Saturday
Jamie—Wednesday

page 46—Shoes and Towels

Jeff—green towel/red sandals

Ted—blue towel/green running shoes

Steve—brown towel/brown loafers

Chris—red towel/blue sneakers

page 50—Sports Fever

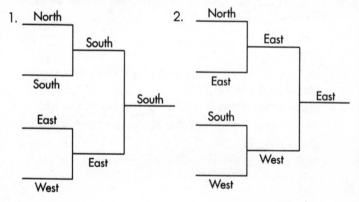

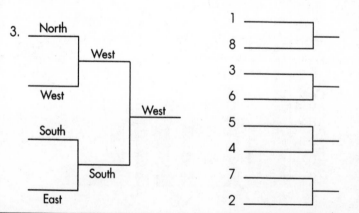

page 47—Houses, Pets and Order

Billy Brown—green house/whale/2nd house
Willy White—blue house/bull/ 3rd house
Bobby Blue—brown house/gorilla/1st house
George Green—white house/bear/4th house

page 51—Meet the Players

Al—guard/black
Bob—forward/white
Carl—forward/black
David—forward/black

Evan—guard/white
Evan is the high scorer.

Answer Key

page 49—Company Communication

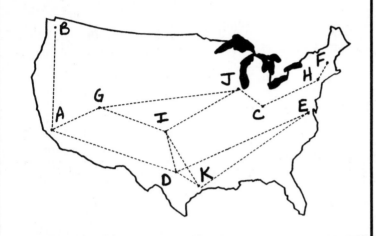

page 52—Patterns I and II

18-7; 17-8; 16-9; 15-1; 14-2; 13-3; 12-4; 11-5; 10-6

a. 36, 42, 48, 54, 60 (add 6)
b. 34, 55, 89, 144, 233 (add the preceeding number)
c. 30, 15, 0, -15, -30 (subtract 15)
d. 12.6, 15.6, 18.6, 21.6, 24.6 (add 3)
e. 41, 38, 35, 32, 29 (subtract 3)
f. 42, 52, 62, 72, 82 (add 10)
g. 11.8, 13.6, 15.4, 17.2, 19 (add 1.8)
h. 1, $1\frac{1}{4}$, $1\frac{1}{2}$, $1\frac{3}{4}$, 2 (add $\frac{1}{4}$)
i. 12.8, 11.1, 9.4, 7.7, 6 (subtract 1.7)
j. 202, 214, 226, 238, 250 (add 12)

pages 54 and 55—Just for Fun! (A)

1.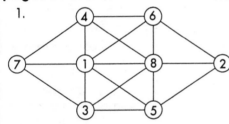
2.

3. Ms. red is wearing white. Ms. White is wearing blue. Ms. Blue is wearing red.
4. Each letter is the first letter of the numbers 1 to 100.
5. He will earn too much for 30 days—over $500,000,000.
6. **Leslie** and **Bill** went to the **zoo**. They walked up a **high hill**. **Leslie** broke the **heel** of her **shoe** when **she** stepped in a **hole**. **She** had to **hobble** around and her **leg** hurt. **Bill** almost stepped on a **goose egg**.
7. Ted—tenth floor; Ally—fourteenth floor; Kathy—eighth floor; Bill—seventh floor
8. Bob—lawyer; Ann—teacher; Carl—pediatrician

page 53—You Grade It!

3. $16\frac{2}{3}$
7. 32'
11. $\frac{8}{9}$
12. $17\frac{1}{2}$
16. 5 ft 7 in.
19. 125%

page 62—Pictures

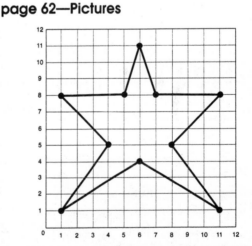

page 58—Map Reading

1. (H, 1)
2. (D, 7)
3. (H, 7)
4. (D, 4)
5. (F, 3)
6. (C, 5)
7. Bellwin
8. Elliot
9. High Valley
10. Farno
11. Waynesville
12. Curan

page 67—Equation-Solving Skills

1. y = -2
2. x = -4
3. a = 15
4. x = -4
5. y = $\frac{1}{2}$
6. x = -4
7. n = -7
8. x = $-\frac{21}{2}$
9. x = -3
10. y = $-\frac{49}{2}$
11. x = -2
12. x = 2

page 68—Make a Table/Draw a Picture

C. $52t + 75t = 635$
$127t = 635$
$t = 5$

Answer: each travels 5 hrs, they will meet in 5 hrs

page 69—Make a Table...

C. $4.00(x) + 5.75(100 - x) = 4.70(100)$
$4x + 575 - 5.75x = 470$
$-1.75x = -105$
$x = 60$
$100 - x = 40$

Answer: 60 kg of M&M's, 40 kg of peanuts for desired mixture

Answer Key

4.

	r	t	D
A	x	3	3x
B	100 + x	3	3(100 + x)

$3x + 3(100 + x) = 4800$
$x = 750$
$100 + x = 850$

1st airplane's rate = 750 km/hr
2nd airplane's rate = 850 km/hr

page 70—Make a Table...

1.

	r	t	D
A	45	t	45t
B	40	t	40t

$45t + 40t = 255$
t = 3 hr

3.

	# grams	% gold	Total Value
A	x	25%	.25x
B	30 – x	55%	.55(30 – x)
mix	30	32%	.32(30)

$.25x + .55(30 - x) = .32(30)$
$x = 23$
$30 - x = 7$

23 grams of 25% gold
7 grams of 55% gold

2.

	# of kilo	Price	Total Value
A	x	$6.00	6.00 (x)
B	20	$3.25	3.25 (20)
mix	x + 20	$4.50	4.50 (x + 20)

$6.00(x) + 3.25(20) = 4.50(x + 20)$
x = 16 ²/₃ kg

5.

	#	Price	Total Value
dimes	x	.10	.10x
nickels	66 – x	.05	.05(66 – x)

$.10x + .05(66 - x) = 5.00$
$x = 34$
$66 - x = 32$

34 dimes, 32 nickels

page 71—Algebraic Geometry

$2x + 2(3x) = 120$
15 meters = width
45 meters = length

page 72—Algebraic Geometry

1.
   x + 4
   x

$2(x) + 2(x + 4) = 40$
8 in. = width
12 in. = length

2.
   2x + 5
   x

$2(x) + 2(2x + 5) = 82$
12 ft = width
29 ft = length

3. 2x + 9
   x

$2(x) + 2(2x + 9) = 174$
26 m = width
61 m = length

4.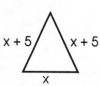
   x + 5   x + 5
   x

$x + (x + 5) + (x + 5) = 37$
3rd side = 9 cm
2 equal sides = 14 cm each

5.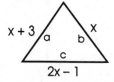
   x + 3   x
   a   b
   c
   2x – 1

$x + (x + 3) + (2x - 1) = 26$
side a = 9
side b = 6
side c = 11

6.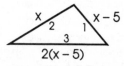
   x   x – 5
   2   1
   3
   2(x – 5)

$x + (x - 5) + 2(x - 5) = 33$
1st leg = 7 km
2nd leg = 12 km
3rd leg = 14 km

page 73—Think About This...

1. 29
2. $1.35 (3 quarters, 5 dimes, 2 nickels)
3. 156 times
4. 22 ft of black, 12 ft of red
5. red = circle, blue = square, green = triangle
6. 5
7. 41 and 32
8. 36 chickens, 18 pigs

page 74—You Grade It! (B)

2. b. $3.25
4. 3/5
5. 39 min 25 sec